PENGUIN BOOKS

TRAVELING LIGHT

Bill Barich's fiction and nonfiction appear regularly in *The New Yorker*, and he has written as well for such diverse publications as *The American Poetry Review*, *Playboy*, and *Sports Illustrated*. His work has been collected in *Best American Short Stories*, *The Ultimate Fishing Book*, *Literary Journalism*, and other anthologies both here and abroad. His previous book, *Laughing in the Hills*, is also published by Penguin Books. He currently lives in northern California.

BILL BARICH
Traveling Light

PENGUIN BOOKS

PENGUIN BOOKS
Viking Penguin Inc., 40 West 23rd Street,
New York, New York 10010, U.S.A.
Penguin Books Ltd, Harmondsworth,
Middlesex, England
Penguin Books Australia Ltd, Ringwood,
Victoria, Australia
Penguin Books Canada Limited, 2801 John Street,
Markham, Ontario, Canada L3R 1B4
Penguin Books (N.Z.) Ltd, 182–190 Wairau Road,
Auckland 10, New Zealand

First published in the United States of America by
The Viking Press 1984
This edition published by Viking Penguin Inc. 1985

LIBRARY OF CONGRESS CATALOGING IN PUBLICATION DATA
Barich, Bill.
   Traveling light.
   Contents: Steelhead on the Russian — Revenge at
Golden Gate fields — J.D. Ross's vision — [etc.]
   1. Voyages and travels — 1951-   .   I. Title.
[G470.B255   1985]   910.4   84-18884
ISBN 0 14 00.7418 X (pbk.)

Printed in the United States of America by
R. R. Donnelley & Sons Company, Harrisonburg, Virginia
Set in Bodoni Book

The author wishes to thank William Shawn
and the checking staff of *The New Yorker*
for their many kindnesses.

All of the essays in this book appeared originally in *The New Yorker* in slightly different
form, with the exception of "O'Neill Among the Weakfish," which appeared originally
in *Sports Illustrated* in different form, under the title "For the Author, Some Weakfish-
ing Strengthened Dormant Family Ties."

Grateful acknowledgment is made to the following for permission to reprint, copy-
righted material:

Harvard University Press: A selection from *A Poet's Journal: Days of 1945–1951*, by
Seferis, 1974.
Penguin Books Ltd: A selection from "Silence" and "My Rivers" from *Giuseppe
Ungaretti: Selected Poems*, translated by Patrick Creagh (Penguin Modern European
Poets, 1971). Translation copyright © 1971 by Patrick Creagh.

for my brother and sister,
fellow travelers,
with love

❧ ❧

Contents

Preface

This book has many happy memories for me. I wrote most of it during eighteen months of spontaneous and sometimes manic travel. The travel was an antidote to an overdose of stability. For better than five years, my wife and I had been living poor in an isolated agricultural valley, north of San Francisco, and I was beginning to talk to the wallpaper. When an editor from New York asked me to contribute a story to a fishing anthology he was putting together, I jumped at the chance and used part of my fee to make a trip to Oregon with a friend of mine to fish for steelhead trout. In Portland, we hired a guide to take us down the Deschutes River. This guide liked to sing. His voice was awful, but that didn't stop him. He sang in sporting goods stores, in his old wooden drift boat, in the camps we made along the river. Here was a person who believed that the soul of Caruso had transmigrated into his bosom. I grew very fond of him, and of the unfamiliar landscape, and I was sorry when the trip was over.

Right after I got back to the valley, a miracle happened: I earned some money on my first book. For a writer, money is always a luxury, so I did the responsible thing and socked mine into a savings bank. Then I went to my room and worked on various projects. The projects were slow to gather steam. I kept thinking about Oregon, about that bad-voiced but liberated little monkey of a guide. To break the monotony, I made a couple of short jaunts—one to Golden Gate Fields racetrack, and the other to the upper Skagit River, in northwestern Washington—and wrote about them for *The New Yorker*. The trips convinced me that as long as the rewards of the world outstripped those of my imagination, I might as well keep traveling. I reclaimed the money and gave notice to the landlord. Our furniture went into storage, courtesy of Allied Van Lines. We grabbed our suitcases, a carton of books, a typewriter, a case of wine, and, unbelievably, a pasta machine, then packed it into our Datsun and headed east.

Over the next year or so, we had three different addresses. We lived on eastern Long Island; in London; and in the Arcetri district, above Florence. There were side trips to upstate New York; to the English countryside; and to Rome, Venice, and Ravenna. Whenever something struck my fancy, I wrote about it; and it's those pieces that make up the bulk of the book. Although they conform in some measure to the specifics of travel-writing, they are perhaps better seen as a record of my preoccupations on the road—friends, family, fishing, horse-racing, history, art, and so on. In general, I did a sad job of seeking out local variants of the Taj Mahal, preferring instead to stick my nose into mundane haunts. I've always felt that the character of any given place is best reflected in its daily routines, so I tended to gravitate toward situations where the most ordinary and familiar activities were going on.

In Italy, our money began to run low. We flew back to California and settled in San Francisco. The transition wasn't easy. Travel spoils you for regular life. When you're moving from country to country in blithe ignorance, you're usually granted the safe passage of a holy idiot. Then, too, everything looks fresh when you're in motion. London is of course drab, bleak, and dirty, but it never *seemed* that way to me. San Francisco, on the other hand, immediately revealed its distractions: traffic noise, barking dogs, amplified disco music, leaks and flaws in our apartment. I knew I'd be living with imperfection for quite some time, so—perversely, against human reason—I started to pine for rural isolation and resurrected an old practice of escaping the city by going into the mountains to fish for trout. "Hat Creek and the McCloud" tells of the trip I made just after our return from Europe. It marks the end of the trail, late autumn 1982.

I've arranged the pieces in chronological order, but there's really no need to read them that way. They are self-contained units, meant to stand on their own legs and entertain. With the exception of "J. D. Ross's Vision," which I wrote as a working reporter, none of the pieces existed first as an idea—that is, I didn't hang around The Fountain so I could do a portrait of a London pub, but because the beer tasted good. The writing came after the fact, as a kind of celebration. For that I owe a debt of thanks to friends, old and new, who led me to experiences I might otherwise not have had. In a few instances, I have changed their names to preserve their anonymity. In the case of "Paul Deeds," who didn't want to be identified at all, I have altered so many details that he is no longer recognizable to his mother. Thanks should also go to my editors, who remained open to receiving unexpected manuscripts from post offices far outside the mainstream.

When I think back over my travels, I feel profoundly lucky. Images from various places keep coming into my mind. The voice I most often hear on the sound track belongs to Giustino, a displaced Italian chef who drank at The Fountain and carried on conversations in a bastard mix of languages. Every Sunday, he went to a street market to shop for the big meal he cooked for his wife, and he liked to show me what he'd bought. He'd yank the food from his shopping bag—vegetables, beefsteak, red wine—and display it on the bar. Then he'd step away to admire the arrangement. This was a version of the cosmos, how it ought to be. "Lovely," Giustino would say, kissing his fingertips. *"Lovely!"* I know of no better description of my time on the road.

ONE

WEST
AND EAST

Allons! the road is before us!
—Walt Whitman, "Song of the Open Road"

Yes, as everyone knows, meditation
and water are wedded forever.
—Herman Melville, *Moby Dick*

❧ ❧

Steelhead
on the Russian

 The river on which I used to live—the Russian, in northern California—was named in honor of the fur traders who established settlements near it almost two centuries ago, beginning in 1812, when Ivan Alexander Kuskoff, a one-legged adventurer employed by the Russian-American Fur Company, leased several acres of coastal land from Pomo Indians, in exchange for blankets, breeches, horses, axes, and some beads. It has its headwaters in the mountains north of Redwood Valley and flows south and west for a hundred and ten miles, to Jenner, on the Pacific Ocean. During the dry summer months, it's a slow, green stream, thick with algae and pestered by canoers. But in November, when the winter rains start, the Russian is transformed: it grows wide and deep and sometimes rises to the limits of its banks and then swamps them, flooding downriver towns like Guerneville and Duncans Mills. It looks majestic at flood stage, seems as broad as the Mississippi. Uprooted trees drift by, along with fences, unmoored boats, rusted agricultural tools, plastics, and hubcaps. If you stand on the cliffs above Jenner and watch the procession of objects sweeping past, you get the feeling that entire communities are being borne

to oblivion on the tide. Seals congregate at the river mouth, dipping into the turbid, muddy water in search of migratory fish. Large numbers of salmon, shad, sturgeon, and striped bass used to ascend the Russian to spawn in its tributaries, but their runs have been badly depleted. The only anadromous ("running upward," in Greek) fish that still persists in any quantity is the steelhead, a subspecies of rainbow trout.

Steelhead are members of the Salmonidae, a family that includes all salmon, trout, and char. They are known scientifically as *Salmo gairdneri*—*Salmo* from the Latin verb meaning "to leap," and *gairdneri* for the nineteenth-century naturalist Meredith Gairdner, who helped Sir John Richardson collect specimens of Columbia River fish for the Hudson's Bay Company. Steelhead have a stronger migratory urge than most rainbow trout but are not dependent on an anadromous existence; if they're planted in a lake, they'll spawn in tributaries of that lake, skipping their saltwater wandering. Most Russian River steelhead opt for anadromy: they're born in freshwater, migrate into the Pacific between their first and third years (at sea, their upper bodies turn steel blue, a change that accounts for their common name), reach sexual maturity in from one to three years more, and return to their natal stream to spawn. They recognize the stream by its unique chemical composition and follow its trail like bloodhounds. Once they've paired off and chosen an instream spawning site, the female digs a redd, or nest, using her body and tail to clear away gravel, then deposits some of her eggs. Immediately, her mate fertilizes them with his milt, a chalky secretion of the reproductive glands. The process is repeated until two thousand eggs have been deposited.

Pacific salmon die after spawning, but some steelhead—perhaps twenty per cent—survive, and may make the journey from ocean to river two, three, or even four times. Steelhead are notoriously elusive at sea. They are seldom snared in a commercial salmon net, although they frequent the same waters as salmon. Nobody knows how they avoid the nets, because marine researchers haven't been able to track them once they enter the Pacific. They disappear—off to the Bering Sea or Baja California or Japan. Anglers find them just about as difficult to catch. In the winter of 1954, the California Department of Fish and Game sponsored a steelhead census among anglers on the Russian; the figures showed that the average angler caught 0.55 fish per day. There are probably fewer steelhead in the river now—the annual run is estimated at about fifty thousand—but the weather in which they thrive hasn't changed: cold, foggy mornings and evenings, relieved on occasion by brilliant afternoon sunshine that warms the bones and stipples the water with light.

I knew nothing about steelhead when I moved into my house in Alexander Valley. I assumed they were neither more nor less intractable than other trout, but I was wrong. The first winter I spent fishing for them proved educational in the extreme. For more hours than I'd care to count, I waited by the river, casting lures into the current and wondering why I never got a strike. In fact, I don't think I would have hooked a fish all season if it hadn't been for Paul Deeds, my friend and mentor. Deeds is a gentle, ordinarily taciturn soul of forty-two who occupies a ramshackle cottage on a thirty-acre prune ranch. He has as little tolerance for pretense as anybody I've ever known. Once, on his birthday, I gave him a reprint edition of Zane Grey's classic *Tales of Fresh-Water Fishing,* which contains a marvelously florid story, "Rocky Riffle," about fishing for steelhead on the Rogue River, in Oregon. The book was a risky gift, because of its pervasive floridness, and also because Deeds is not much of a reader—he sticks to the evening paper and supermarket scandal sheets. He thanked me for the book, then leafed through it and looked at the pictures, stopping when he came to one that showed Grey, in a flat-brimmed hat, cavorting on a snowy hillside with three bears. The photograph was captioned, THE BEARS ON THE WAY TO CRATER LAKE—TAME, BUT NOT VERY!

"What's this got to do with steelhead?" Deeds asked.

I explained that Grey, like Jack London or Ernest Hemingway, was a larger-than-life character.

"You can't be larger than life," said Deeds. "That's a contradiction in terms. Here, listen to this stuff. 'The steelhead lay flat on the gravel. I stared, longing for the art of the painter, so as to perpetuate the exquisite hues and contours of that fish. All trout are beautiful. But this one of sea species seemed more than beautiful. He gaped, he quivered.' "

"You've got to take it with a grain of salt, Paul," I said. "It's from another era."

Deeds closed the book, smiled superciliously, and flipped over the record on his turntable. He has a vast collection of blues albums, ranging from Bessie Smith, through B. B. King, to John Mayall. I was forced to listen to most of it the first time I met him, back in mid-December of my frustrating educational winter. He helped me regain my sanity. I'd become something of a steelhead monk, locked into an unvarying—and unproductive—routine. Every day, I woke at dawn, built a small fire in the Ashley stove, ate a solitary breakfast of shredded wheat and tea, and dressed in my fishing uniform: jeans, turtleneck, flannel shirt, Pendleton jacket, two pairs of woolen socks, and a black-knit watch cap. Outside the house, I put on my waders and cinched them with a belt, buckling it tight as a precautionary measure against seepage in case I fell into the water—something I'd done often in the past. From my available gear, I'd assembled a kitful of lures and a makeshift steelhead rig— an eight-foot fiberglass rod and a medium-sized spinning reel wound with twelve-pound test—and I took it in hand and walked off into a seemingly static landscape that could have been painted by Hokusai: twisted live oak trees, barren willows, new winter grass, and vineyards laced with yellow mustard flowers, everything cloaked in river mist.

In spite of this ritual behavior, I didn't even see a steelhead, much less get a bite, until I ran into Deeds. This happened about eleven o'clock one bitter-cold morning, while I was taking a break from my listless casting. I was sitting on a strip of sand and blowing on my numb fingertips when I heard noises in the brush behind me—the scuffing of rubber boots over pebbles and then a hacking cough. Deeds emerged from the trees. His beard was moist with drizzle; he was wiping his wet lips on his sleeve. When he noticed me, his eyes widened in murderous circles, because he was unaccustomed to seeing strangers.

I told him I'd just rented the old Fratelli place.

"You rented it?" he asked incredulously. "You rented it, and you like to fish?"

He seemed crestfallen at the idea of competition. But after we had talked for a while, and he realized that I was a rank amateur, he was much more accommodating and pleasant, and I invited him to come up to the house for lunch.

"Wait a minute," he said. He vanished into the willows and returned with a steelhead he'd caught that morning. The fish weighed nine pounds or so—about average for the Russian. It was a steel blue along the spine; below, it had a bright silver color, which camouflaged it from ocean predators.

"Male or female?" I asked.

"Female," said Deeds. "Look at her mouth. See how nice and round it is? Bucks, they have hooked jaws."

"Has she been in the river long?"

"Nah, she's fresh-run. She'd be much darker and have a red streak on her side. She hasn't spawned yet. Feel," he said.

He jabbed my finger into the steelhead's belly. It was hard and protuberant, full of eggs. There were some gashes above the ventral fins, and I asked about them.

"Sea lion almost got her," Deeds said.

At the house, I gave him a bourbon while I made a couple of roast-beef sandwiches. The bourbon was a bad mistake. Deeds seldom drinks, because liquor unleashes torrential energies in him. He rambles on and on, discussing stride piano or prune horticulture or other esoterica, then suddenly loses his near-pathological fear of travel—ordinarily, he hates to leave the valley, even for emergencies—and decides that the best thing to do under the circumstances is to jump into the pickup and drive right to Reno, preferably at ninety miles an hour. But I didn't know this at the time. We ate the sandwiches, along with pickles, coleslaw, and a few underripe winter tomatoes, and had another drink, and then Deeds slapped his palm on the table and insisted that I visit his cottage, immediately.

We went over there. I was not prepared for the disarray—clothing covered most of the available furniture. In the living room, a large golden retriever named Honey was stretched out on a divan, gnawing audibly on a steak bone. Deeds patted her, dropped his coat on the floor, and led me into the kitchen. He spread some pages from the *Star* on the counter, slit the steelhead's belly, and removed her roe. It peeled away in two pearly, salmon-pink slabs, which Deeds dusted with borax, then double-wrapped in cellophane and aluminum foil.

"Best bait there is," he said, stuffing the package into the refrigerator and simultaneously extracting two beers. He told me how he shaped the roe into "berries": he cut a fingernail-size chunk from one of the slabs, set it on a two-inch square of maline—a fine red mesh material that blends with the roe—and then twisted the maline tight at the top and tied it securely with red thread. The finished product resembled a strawberry. "You got to fish 'em on a gold hook," he said. "Otherwise, you're wasting your time."

"Why do steelhead strike their own roe?"

"Cannibal instinct."

"Do you ever use flies instead of bait?"

"Listen," he said. "I'd rather fly-fish than anything. But the river's too high and discolored most of the time. If you want action, you go with bait."

We went back into the living room, and Deeds brought down a quart of Jim Beam from an antique highboy. The bottle had spiderwebbing trailing from its cap; the tiny faces on the label were faded from the sun. I don't recall very much after this, although I know I stayed for dinner. Deeds fed me steelhead. I watched in awe as he concocted his special barbecue sauce—mayo, ketchup, A.1., Lea & Perrins, brown sugar, onions, garlic, and corn relish—and slathered it on the skinned fish, then jammed the whole reeking mess under the broiler. It tasted fine, though—at least, to my numbed palate.

After the meal, Deeds embarked on a lengthy monolog about the demise of the Russian River. He showed me some photographs in support of his case; they would have done Zane Grey proud. "That's 1964," he said, pointing to three big steelhead arranged on a bed of ferns. "I caught them in thirty minutes. You won't see that happen again. Too much *junk* in the river. Chemicals. Garbage. Sewage. Damn kids drive their dune buggies down the creek beds, right through the water. Can you imagine that? They run over steelhead fry. Death by tires. It's incredible. I'm talking about *incredible.* Don't they understand that creek beds are out of bounds? Only fish that are in the river are fair game." His mood became elevated again when he brought down a second bottle of Beam. He showed me a few more pictures—all of his former wife, from whom he'd been recently divorced—and then said, "I'll bet you'd like to hear some music," and proceeded to play his way through the blues collection. When I left, shortly after midnight, he was using his rod tip like a baton to conduct a medley of Howlin' Wolf tunes.

I didn't expect to see Deeds for a few days—not in the wake of such carousing—but he came by the next afternoon and apologized for not offering me a ride home.

"You offered, Paul," I said, "but you wanted to go through Reno first."

Deeds laughed. "I meant to give you these," he said, digging into his pocket and handing over a jar containing five berries. "And these"—an assortment of lead weights. "And these"—three twenty-five-pound-test leaders. Each leader had a knot in it, so it could be attached to a regular monofilament by means of a swivel. Below the knot, the leaders were divided into two uneven strands. "You tie your weight on the short one," he said. "You want it to bounce along the river bottom, down where the fish are. Not too fast and not too slow—tick, tick, tick." He was demonstrating with an invisible rod, keeping his eyes fixed on the line. "The bait follows behind. If you feel the bait stop, wham!"—he jerked back the rod—"you set up. That drives the barb of the hook through the fish's lip."

"How should I play the fish?"

"With steelhead, you don't play," said Deeds. "You pray."

That evening, just as the sky was turning, I stationed myself near a deep pool below a rocky outcrop and started casting. Deeds's weights were much heavier than the lures I'd been using. The one I tied to the shorter strand of leader bounced properly on the bottom—tick, tick, tick, like seconds passing. Suddenly, the berry stopped in transit, as if a fish had mouthed it. I lifted my rod, preparing to do battle, but I felt no resistance. Soon enough, I reeled in a fat sucker; it flopped onto the shore like a sack of mush. Suckers are trash fish, insults to divinity. They have chubby humanoid lips and appear to be begging for cigars. It's possible to envision them wearing suspenders and sitting on park benches, acting like heirs to the continent's watershed. I released mine, stifling a desire to kick it, and moved toward the center of the pool. I put my next cast under some willows on the opposite shore. Tick, tick, tick: again the bait stopped, and again I set the hook. This time, a steelhead shot out of the water. I played, or prayed, the fish for ten minutes, certain that I'd lose it, but my luck held, and I was able finally to draw it into the shallows and beach it. The fish was small, about four pounds, and male; so much milt leaked from him that a white puddle formed on the sand. I dispatched him quickly, suffused with guilt, but the guilt changed to atavistic pride once I had threaded a willow branch through his mouth and out of his gills and begun the uphill trek to my house. I stopped on a rise and looked back at the valley, which was vanishing in purple haze. As Zane Grey put it, "the sunset was beautiful, resembling ships of silver clouds with rosy sails that crossed the lilac sea of sky in the west."

Deeds became my nemesis as well as my friend. Never again would he grant me the license of undisturbed water. If I was fishing, he was fishing, too—often just ahead of me, combing the better pools and riffles before I had a chance at them. The situation would have been intolerable if I hadn't continued to learn from him. He persuaded me to buy a longer, sturdier rod and a bait-casting reel; taught me to use bobbers in bright red, pink, and chartreuse to attract fish;

instructed me in the basics of steelhead anatomy; and gave me a short course in how to cast a shooting head—a twenty-eight-to-thirty-foot-long, single-tapered line that allows an angler to cast great distances without exerting much effort.

That first winter, I caught ten fish; they were poached, baked, broiled, eaten as sashimi, or soaked in brine and then smoked over hickory chips until their flesh was glazed and peeled away in savory chunks. Deeds caught forty-six; most were released, but a few prime specimens were subjected to the ignominy of his barbecue sauce. I thought my statistics would improve the following winter, but California entered a two-year drought, and steelhead fishing was dismal. When the drought ended, the rains were exceptionally heavy, and the Russian remained high, muddy, and inaccessible for most of the season. The year after *that,* rainfall did taper off, and the river was in excellent shape, but fish were scarce, because the drought had affected spawning adversely. In the low, clear water, steelhead eggs and fry had been more vulnerable than ever to predators, and the mortality rate had been increased by soaring temperatures and a poor supply of oxygen. I tried to be hopeful, but in mid-September, right before the *next* (depressing? suicidal?) season was to begin, I cracked. I had a little money coming from a writing job, so I said to Deeds, who was helping himself to my good French-roast coffee, "I can't take it anymore, Paul. I'm going to Oregon for some real fishing."

"I'll go with you," Deeds said.

I doubted his sincerity. "You dare to leave California?"

"I've done it before," he said defensively.

It happened that he had a sister in Portland, who had been hounding him to visit. Her name was Joan, and she met us at the airport. She was a big woman, built like Deeds, with bony shoulders and elbows. She was ten years older than he was, and the age difference showed in their relationship. She had a tendency to treat him in a mock-scolding manner, as if he were a bad boy in need of constant correction; he responded by acting petulant and making snide comments. It was all very stylized, a residue of childhood. Her husband, a machinist, told us he cared nothing about fishing. "If I want salmon," he said jovially, "I go to the supermarket." I suppose most families seem odd when they're viewed from the outside. I made some phone calls while this family did its catching up, and arranged for a guide to take Paul and me on a three-day drift trip down the Deschutes River. The Deschutes is a legendary steelhead stream, known for its productivity; the lower portion, which we'd be drifting, is wild and free-flowing. The guide assured me that the river would be perfect for fly-fishing, unless we got some rain. I had a good night's sleep in the guest room and spent the next day buying tackle in Portland's sporting-goods stores. I wanted to rent a car, too, but Joan insisted that I save the money; she volunteered to drive us to Maupin, where we were to launch the boat, and then pick us up at the mouth of the Deschutes—it empties into the Columbia River—at the end of the trip.

We got an early start in the morning. I tried my best to ease the tension between Deeds and his sister. I made jokes, and even did some whistling, but their bickering never quit. About ten o'clock, we stopped for huckleberry pancakes at a restaurant near Mt. Hood, and then we descended into a desert atmosphere of dry, brown hills and clumps of sage.

"Zane Grey country, Paul," I said.

Deeds felt better when we reached Maupin. The guide was waiting for us outside a bar, holding a can of Blitz beer in his hand. His wooden drift boat—pale green, about thirteen feet long, with a slightly elevated prow—was attached to a trailer hitch and stacked high with supplies, to which we added our rods, tackle, sleeping bags, liquor, and sundries. We launched the boat at a ramp about a mile downstream from the bar. The Deschutes isn't really treacherous, except in its last five miles or so, when it drops briskly in elevation to join the Columbia, and four sets of rapids are created, but I still experienced a few seconds' panic as we were tugged forward into the current. I was aware of the river's power, of its swiftness, and of land falling irretrievably away behind us. The trip took on aspects of a childhood adventure. We drifted around a bend and into more primitive terrain: no cars, roads, or people, just craggy buttes and rattlesnakes and dust.

The guide worked his oars to keep us on the edges of the white water. He'd navigated the Deschutes a thousand times and claimed to know where the fish would be. "I don't guarantee they'll cooperate," he said. "Only that they'll be in attendance." As we passed one likely riffle after another, we became fidgety and fumbled with our rods. Deeds lit a cigarette; I had a nip of whiskey. Finally, the guide stopped near a moderately fast stretch that seemed the perfect habitat for steelhead. We were out of the boat before its prow touched the ground. I had trouble keeping my balance at first. I listed to the left in concord with the river's flow, drawn unavoidably in its governing direction.

Deeds beat me to the water, of course, and, after a false cast or two, laid out thirty feet of weight-forward floating fly line. We were both using nine-foot rods and a wet fly I'd bought in Portland—a Skykomish Sunrise. The fly was a beauty. It was supposed to represent the colors of a sunrise along the Skykomish River, in Washington—red, yellow, and silver, dressed with white bucktail wings on a No. 4 hook. I'm sure I chose the fly for its metaphoric content rather than for its resemblance to a bait fish or a bit of free-floating roe. I was particularly susceptible to aesthetic considerations when I was buying flies. Once, I'd filled a paper sack with tiny jassids, because they reminded me of Egyptian scarabs. I never caught a fish with any of them. Probably, I would never catch a fish with my Skykomish Sunrise, but it pleased me to watch it cut through the clear water, just beneath the surface. I asked the guide if the fly should run deeper. No, he said—the steelhead would come up to take it if they were curious enough. Deeds was working the slicks about twenty yards above me. I imitated his style: cast, quarter the line, retrieve, take two steps to the left. We must have looked like a comedy dance team practicing for the Elks' annual picnic. Deeds was concentrating so hard he didn't hear the guide announce that we were moving to another spot. I had to wade over and tap him on the shoulder. "What is it?" he asked irritably, his eyes hard behind the tinted lenses of his glasses.

Late that afternoon, in some frothy riffles, I nailed our first steelhead on a Deschutes Skunk, a dry fly that the guide had lent me. The Skunk was sparsely tied and didn't ride as high on the water as dries ordinarily do. The fish inhaled it on the retrieve, with such abandon that I almost lost control of my rod. I managed to tighten my grip before the rod escaped, and I passed the next quarter hour dashing back and forth along the bank, following the steelhead when it made its runs. The runs were long and dramatic, often punctuated by aerial high jinks. I should have cupped my hand around my reel to provide some drag—the necessary resistance—but I hadn't played many steelhead on a fly rod, so I didn't realize this, and compensated by jogging. Deeds thought the jogging was very funny, and he laughed. He laughed even harder when the guide started jogging behind me, waving around a landing net. No doubt the guide would have been laughing, too, but I hadn't paid him yet; he was forced to maintain his professional composure. Gradually, the fish began to tire, and I drew him toward the shallows, where the guide scooped him up—a six-pound buck whose dorsal fin was stubby and malformed.

"Hatchery fish," the guide said, touching the fin. "They rub up against each other in the holding tanks and bite off each other's fins."

I wiped the sweat from my brow and glanced at Deeds; his laughter had turned to envy.

We set up camp that evening in a grove of alders. The buttes across the water were red; the water itself was dissolving in blackness. I shucked off my waders and did some stretching exercises, glad to be free of constriction. Deeds brewed coffee in a dented tin pot; the guide and I shared the bourbon. "You gentlemen are lucky," the guide said after his third drink, "for I am an excellent cook." Indeed he was, in the grand campground tradition of abundance. He filleted the steelhead, then broiled it over a wood fire and served it with skillet-fried potatoes and a tossed green salad. We applauded his culinary skills and awarded him another bourbon. Magpies flitted about over the camp, diving now and again into the sage. "Dessert, gentlemen," the guide said, serving us wedges of Sara Lee cheesecake on pink paper plates. The moon appeared over the buttes. It was almost full and shed a soft, pale light that rippled on the ripples of the water. The guide washed his pots in a plastic basin, singing a many-versed song about love and death in the wilderness. I awarded him a final bourbon, on the condition that he drink it in silence, and unrolled my sleeping bag near Deeds. I woke just once during the night, when a Union Pacific freight train wailed in the distance. The sound was so melancholy it gave me the chills. It was like somebody weeping in a darkened theater long after the movie's ended. I sat up and looked at the moon and the smoke rising from the fire.

The guide nudged me at dawn. "Fishing time," he said.

I had no melancholy left—only aching bones and sore joints. Deeds was polishing the lenses of his glasses with a dish towel. He put on his waders and vest and walked into the river. I followed him. I could see the sun shining on the ridges of the buttes, but down there in the canyon it was still cold and gray. Two steps and cast, two steps and cast—we took thirty fishless steps before the guide called us to breakfast. After eating, we broke camp, drifted downstream for a mile or so, and waded into the water again. By three in the afternoon, we'd hooked five steelhead, and had released all but one—the dinner fish. "I feel pretty damn decent," said Deeds, resting on the shore. He has the country person's compactness of expression, saving his superlatives for truly earth-shattering events, like wars, hurricanes, famines, and the failure of his pickup to start on demand.

That evening, we had our fish poached in wine and chicken broth. At Deeds's request, I read aloud from *Tales of Fresh-Water Fishing.* I chose a passage describing a nine-pound Rogue River buck:

He looked exactly what he was, a fish-spirit incarnate, fresh run from the sea, with opal and pearl hues of such delicate loveliness that no pen or brush could portray them. He brought the sea with him and had taken on the beauty of the river. He had a wild savage head, game as that of an eagle, jaws of a wolf, eyes of black jewel, full of mystic fire.

"Very ripe," said Deeds, chewing contentedly on a cheroot.

"Jaws of a wolf?" the guide asked. "Full of mystic fire?"

We took three more fish on our last day, not counting a giant that Deeds lost—a huge steelhead that sounded three times, made a crazed run upstream, and snapped Deeds's leader at the tippet. Usually, that would have thrown Deeds into a funk, but this time he accepted his fate with equanimity. He even smiled a little. The smile was rueful, haunted. "You'll get the bastard next trip," the guide said. "Jay-sus, what a monster!" He advised us to fasten the clasps on our life jackets, because the Deschutes was dropping quickly and we were about to shoot the rapids.

White water loomed ahead—great furls of it. Boulders

were visible in the spume. "I'm going to have to pay attention here for a minute," the guide said, working his oars to position us. The roar of the water grew louder and louder. I looked at Deeds; he had his fingers in his ears. My muscles tensed involuntarily. I held tightly to the seat. "Wooden boat's more trouble than those rubber rafts," the guide said. "If we hit a rock, we splinter." The current accelerated, pulling us ahead with a vengeance; then we were sucked forward into the gush and tumble and expelled a few seconds later on the other side. The guide brushed some water off his nose. "Gentlemen," he said, "we have cheated death." He negotiated the next three rapids with the same sort of understated flair, keeping us in quiet pockets in the surging foam. The sensation, I thought, must be akin to the one that surfers get when they're riding inside the curl of a wave. I felt protected, enclosed in a husk of space. After the final rapid, the noise level diminished and the river widened by degrees, and we saw people fishing along the shore. The guide drew in his oars, and we glided effortlessly toward the Columbia.

We reached the landing about noon. I paid the guide, awarded him a congratulatory snort, and helped Deeds unload the gear. Joan was waiting for us in the parking lot. I think we frightened her, stomping to the car all sunburned and exuding primitive energies. But this may be a masculine conceit; it's equally possible that she was just offended by our dirty clothes and—in my case—unshaven cheeks. She and Deeds began arguing right away. She wanted him to wrap the steelhead steaks in newspaper before putting them in the cooler; he said that newspaper was unnecessary—that the plastic bags would keep them just fine. Then a serene look crossed his face. "No, Joan," he said. "You're right. I'll unwrap them."

We unwrapped them later that night and cooked them in Joan's kitchen. Her husband was impressed. "These are as good as the market kind," he said. I coughed, and a bit of garlicky butter dribbled down my chin. Later, I sat in a lawn chair on the porch and watched the traffic drift by: round headlights and fluttering moths. Deeds joined me after a while. He'd taken a bath, and his skin smelled incongruously of the perfumed soap he'd borrowed from his sister. He lit a cigarette, and cupped his hand and used it as an ashtray. This was a civilized gesture to make, but a sudden breeze came up and ruined everything by scattering ashes all over the furniture. "We should never have left the river," he said, flipping his cigarette butt into the yard.

Deeds's words were prophetic. We descended from the sublimity of the Deschutes into unseasonably warm weather that promised another drought. During it, I consulted a biologist about the future of the steelhead in the Russian. We met in his office at the California Department of Fish and Game, in Yountville. Behind him on a shelf were several jars containing specimens of fish commonly found in California streams——bass, squawfish, even suckers. The specimens were bleached and rubbery-looking, as though they'd been made in Hong Kong for the express purpose of filling large jars in offices. When I stared at the jars, I perceived a sort of whiteness. I don't know how else to put it: *a whiteness.*

The biologist told me first about salmon and their evolutionary efficiency—how in their run upstream to spawn they literally consume themselves, digesting even the protein in their scales in an effort to continue. Salmon fingerlings are nourished by microorganisms that feed off the corpses of spawned-out elders, in a macabre yet elegant loop. Because salmon have attained such perfection, they cannot easily adapt to changes in their environment, whereas steelhead, being less highly evolved, are more malleable. But this doesn't insure the steelhead's survival in coastal rivers, the biologist said. A myriad factors combine to threaten the fish with extinction: poor timbering practices, which cause erosion and siltation; pollution, both industrial and agricultural; gravel extraction from creeks and streams; development, and the demand it places on the watershed; dams; greater fishing pressure; and so on, through a catalog of familiar woes. The steelhead trout was not an endangered species, but its existence at present was decidedly precarious.

I conveyed none of this information to Deeds. He was already morose and taciturn. One evening, he informed me that he was thinking of selling his land to some pinhead (his word) from the city, thereby earning an enormous profit, which would let him relocate in the Pacific Northwest— probably in Washington, not Oregon, because Joan was in Oregon and, though he loved her dearly, he could not abide sharing a state with her.

"Why not Canada?" I asked. "Why not a cabin on the Babine River? You could eat berry pies and talk to the loons."

He grumbled something about pissant fishermen and played his Bessie Smith album, rather loudly.

A few days later, I saw a realtor's car parked in front of his house. I phoned him that night and asked if he was serious about selling. "I don't wish to discuss it," he said, hanging up. I lost touch with him then.

In October, the first frost hit the valley. The grapevines performed their annual elegiac wilt, as brilliantly as maples. The month of November was unusually dry, but on December 2nd a huge storm roared in from the coast. The sky was dark and ominous for hours. Then five inches of rain fell, and the creeks started flowing. Early the next morning, Deeds knocked at my door. He was wearing a yellow slicker and an old-fashioned rain hat of the type favored by New England sea captains. He invited me to accompany him to Jenner. We drove there in his truck, with the wind blowing intermittent showers across the glass, filling the cab with the scent of fecund earth. We parked above the river; junk and scuds of foam drifted toward the Pacific. There were sea lions at the river mouth. "I had an offer on my place," Deeds said, "but, with all this early rain, you know, we could have a terrific season." I agreed. It was the best thing to do. Dire prophecies were swept to sea; the steelhead were returning.

Revenge at
Golden Gate Fields

Horseplayers are like old soldiers. They never forget the terrain of losing battles. A map of it gets tattooed into their skin. The tattoo I had of Golden Gate Fields was on the order of Queequeg's decoration, covering almost every inch of my body. I'd once holed up at the Terrace Motel on central but inelegant San Pablo Avenue, a stone's throw from the track over in Albany, California, and had spent ten spring weeks trying to sort out my life and simultaneously beat the horses. The life-sorting went pretty well, but the horses refused to cooperate. Their behavior was strange and idiosyncratic; it didn't conform to any of the systems I devised to handicap them. I proved to be a first-rate loser, capable of betting an entire nine-race card without having any of my choices finish in the money. That wasn't easy to take. At the end of the season, I vowed never to return to Golden Gate, but, as they say, vows are made for breaking, and when the steelhead fishing on the Russian was once again disastrous, I found myself tooling down the highway toward Albany on the opening day of the midwinter meeting.

My excuse was that I was honoring a promise to some

friends——a writer and his wife who'd asked me on several occasions if I'd go with them to the track. Neither of them had ever been before, so once we were in our grandstand seats, I wasted about an hour instructing them in the basics. I didn't mind doing it, but it put an added stress on my already fragmentary consciousness. I had no time to consult the *Daily Racing Form* and made my daily-double bets in a daze. The tickets I later held in my hand were a record of anxiety——of the lack of grace under pressure. I could have plucked them at random from a trash can, and probably should have, because I was soon out thirty bucks.

The writer was doing fine, of course. Racetracks seem to reward innocence. If babies were permitted to wager, they'd ultimately win so much money that management everywhere would bar them. NO BABIES ALLOWED, says a big sign at Hialeah. At Belmont Park, it reads, BEAT IT, BABIES. Anyway, I bumped into the writer just as he was collecting eighteen dollars on a two-dollar bet. Happiness beamed forth from his bearded countenance, and his fingers fumbled with slick new greenbacks. The sight upset me, and I did something fiendish. "Why don't you put it all on some horse in the next race?" I asked, insinuating by my tone of voice that any die-hard plunger would feed the excess back into the machine.

The writer is an intrepid fellow——he'd searched through Mexican jungles for the ghost of B. Traven——and he made an on-the-spot selection and shoved his money toward an abashed ticket seller. Maybe the writer's gesture was really bravado, and hence lacking in the necessary innocence, because his horse lost. I still felt guilty about prodding him, though. In atonement, I guess, I started betting dumb hunches, which sent forty bucks more spiraling down the chute. After the seventh race, I was fed up, and I talked everybody into leaving early. We went over to Spenger's Fish Grotto, across the freeway, but even the sweet fresh clams and oysters couldn't sway me from an unalterable sense of defeat. It seemed that I was destined to repeat my mistakes over and over again, with the grievous alacrity of a novice.

For nearly a month after this episode, I sat at home and moped, refusing to even look at a racing paper. The more I moped, the angrier I got. Why was I letting the track push me around? My waffling attitude cast me in the role of victim. I always approached the betting windows too timidly, as if I wanted to ask a favor. Once you've isolated a flaw in your handicapping technique, it's easy to view it as a flaw in your character, too, and I did, recalling timid incidents from my past. The faces of beautiful girls I'd failed to ask out in high school loomed above me in accusatory fashion, followed by the faces of obnoxious people I'd meant to tell off, and then by the sad equine faces of good horses I'd neglected in order to play improbable renegade nags. I saw my whole life as a form of missed experience, of chances dispersed in the wind. I am as open to self-pity as the next person, and I fell to it now with a vengeance, until one night, in the throes of despair, I vowed—another vow!—to go back to Golden Gate and teach it that I wasn't going to be bullied anymore.

I picked a Friday for my return trip. The morning was limpid, auspicious, spoked with rays of sun. I bought a *Form* downtown and read it over breakfast. I could see immediately that the track was planning to make things tough. A horse named Fitch Mountain was entered in the first race. I knew the actual Fitch Mountain quite well, having lived near it for almost five years. It's a cone-shaped mound that should really be called a hill. There's nothing spectacular about Fitch Mountain, but I had a sentimental attachment to it, and I was afraid the attachment would carry over to the horse and force me to bet with my emotions again. I wanted to avoid sloppy emotional errors at all costs. My strategy, such as it was, depended on a hard-nosed belief in simple cause and effect. Things got trickier, and even more tempting, when I noticed who owned Fitch Mountain—a member of the Pedroncelli family, in Geyserville, whose jug wines I sometimes drank.

Fortunately, I was able to exercise some control. I glanced away from all the intriguing names and connections, and examined instead Fitch Mountain's past performances. He had turned in a fair race and a few nice workouts recently, but he didn't compare with a more talented speedster, Al Who. On the basis of the figures, Al Who appeared to be the *Form*'s classic "candidate for graduation"—easily the strongest horse in a field of maidens. (Maidens are horses who've yet to win a race.) I was determined to play him, no matter how seductively Fitch Mountain tugged at my heartstrings.

I walked through a turnstile at Golden Gate at a little past noon. The grandstand was not as packed as it had been on opening day. Dreams of million-dollar exactas had been filed away until next winter. The grounds looked clean and tidy. I wondered if somebody's aunt had taken up residence in the janitorial suite. The restaurants and snack bars had expanded their line of wares since my internship, and now offered fancy items like hand-carved pastrami sandwiches and cream-topped cups of Irish coffee. It was funny to watch bedraggled touts balance the plastic cups like bone china on the palms of their ink-stained hands. Even the racing strip seemed to be in better shape. At the paddock, I overheard a trainer say that it was the best surface he'd run stock on in a year or so, softer and more yielding than the strips in southern California, which are fast but can be hard on horses' legs.

I should probably have avoided the paddock, since it's where the most dangerous flirtations occur. Time and again, I've fallen for gleaming horses only to see them lose their shine as soon as they stepped into the starting gate. I was trying to resist Fitch Mountain, but he looked awfully good, brushed up and tossing his mane like a competitor. Al Who was less impressive. He had the muscular, vaguely criminal look of a retired boxer who's been hanging around the Mob. I just couldn't bet him—it would be like endorsing something corrupt. I couldn't bet Fitch Mountain, either, not after vowing to be serious. Instead, I scanned the *Form* once more—rather desperately now, with post time minutes away—and succumbed to paranoia. Every number was part of a code; every word had at least three meanings. The charts began to slip and slide before my eyes, and from their elliptical jumble I developed a bizarre theory that a thirty-to-one shot was going to steal the purse.

I will not dignify this nag by mentioning his name. He had

been shipped up from Santa Anita, and that gave him (I thought) a touch of class. Roberto Gonzalez, a top jockey, had been engaged to ride him, and I interpreted this as another indication that a real bid was in the offing. Would Gonzalez's agent accept a worthless mount? I doubted it. I became convinced that a conspiracy to make a killing was under way, and I wanted a piece of the action.

When I placed my bet, I did so with an intimation of superior intelligence, but the race was horrible to watch. My conspiracy theory went up in smoke quite early, along with any notions of superior intelligence, when the nag in question failed to leave the gate until after all the other horses had left. This was certainly a polite gesture on the nag's part, but it didn't improve his chances, especially since he'd also broken in the air. His front legs flailed about. He seemed to be climbing an invisible ladder, and was firmly out of contention before the first quarter of the race was over. From his position at the rear of the field, he couldn't even see the leader—predictably, Al Who. Old Mr. Who was sprinting clear, several lengths beyond everybody else. As for Fitch Mountain, he was smack in the middle of the fray, keeping just off the pace but making no attempt to challenge. Fitch Mountain was miles ahead of the Santa Anita nag, suggesting that an emotional wager was better than a paranoid one. It was simple to figure what Al Who represented in such a scheme: Logic. The Big L was always a front-runner. It drove a BMW because of the high resale value, got to the supermarket early to take advantage of unadvertised specials, and kept its shoes polished in anticipation of a visit from the boss. But, for all its preparedness, Logic did not necessarily *obtain* in every situation—it had a nasty habit of collapsing. Favorites (the logical choices) seldom win more than a third of the races at any major track, so it came as no surprise when Al Who faltered in the stretch, and was passed by Shado Matt and Bobo's Prince. Al Who was just conforming to type, disappointing brokers, bankers, and positivists, even as the Santa Anita nag was destroying the intricately constructed fantasies of suckers like me.

After the race, I exiled myself to a cold, dark, inhospitable corner of the grandstand. The afternoon was young, but I was old. Why did I continue to overcomplicate the transparently simple? I'd done it all my life, courting revelation in the most trivial of exchanges. That the world was neither more nor less than it appeared to be was an idea I'd yet to grasp. No doubt a few centuries on an analyst's couch could cure me of my stranglehold on coincidence and synchronism, but I was a little pressed for time. Already the entrants in the second race were being led by their grooms from the barns to the paddock, disclosing with each step subtle aspects of their potential.

I liked Kona Gold, who'd been running poorly of late, because I'd noticed something interesting in his past performances. Last year, his trainer, Eldon Hall, had sent him off in a couple of long route races over a mile and three-sixteenths for which the horse had seemed ill-suited. Kona Gold had done a rotten job in those races, but they'd helped to build up his wind. After Hall rested him, Kona Gold had come back to win handily at a shorter distance—a mile and one-sixteenth. Hall seemed to be repeating the tactic this year:

Kona Gold's recent trouncings had occurred in long routes; he'd rested for about a month; and he was entered in a race at the distance he preferred. I thought the horse couldn't lose. Other bettors didn't agree. They'd made Sterling Drive the favorite, and I understood why. Sterling Drive had suffered bad racing luck his last time out. He'd gotten caught in a tangle, blocked from his purpose. Moreover, he was from a hot stable, and he was taking a nose dive in class for the present race. I had to admit that the horse looked good on paper. It would have required only a minor imaginative leap for me to join Sterling Drive's supporters, but, for once, I held temptation at bay and stuck with my own reasonably substantiated version of the actual. I put thirty bucks on Kona Gold to win, somehow managing to bite my tongue in the process.

Given the historical bias of my wager, I should have been able to watch the race dispassionately, with a kind of Viconian calm, but I was up and dancing on my toes even before the track announcer shouted "They're off!" Sterling Drive broke from the rail, with infinite care, and headed directly for the parking lot, going so wide on the first turn that several fans groaned. "I need a Bromo," said a chunky, dispirited man as he deposited a handful of tickets on the floor. I was treating my own ticket like a splinter of the True Cross, because Kona Gold was sitting right where I want my horse to sit in a route race—third, on the outside, and moving steadily forward. There was something inexorable in his progress. He was three lengths ahead at the top of the stretch, but he kept accelerating anyway, hammering a wedge of merciless space between himself and the other horses, and finished seven lengths in front. Sterling Drive loped in last, as gangly-legged as a cartoon horse, while I attempted to calculate how much I'd earned.

Kona Gold's victory gave me confidence and also a rekindled tolerance for statistics. I slashed through the third-race entrants in the *Form,* discarding horses who would previously have attracted me with their names. I had no use anymore for clever rhymes (Jolly by Golly) or bad puns (The Long Ranger). The flagrant romance of Color Me Dashing left me cold. Even the exotic Palapa—mangoes, grass skirts, rum in coconut shells—failed to entice me. Only two horses really had a chance. The first, Palace Arena, had been close in his last three starts, but the second, Mr. B.F., who'd run in tougher company, far outclassed him. Mr. B.F.'s drawback was that he'd been out of action for eleven months, and I decided to look him over before parting with any of my cash.

Judging a horse by its appearance is one of the most underrated of handicapping skills. The Chinese who frequent Golden Gate seem particularly adept at it. They wait patiently by the paddock fence, smoking unfiltered cigarettes and registering anatomical fine points. They discuss the passing flesh like traders. Arguments about the relative merits of stock are not infrequent. Once, I watched an Oriental man in a shiny black suit as he watched the horses. He held a pencil in his right hand and a program in his left. At three-minute intervals, he lifted the pencil and scratched a name off his list. The mark he made was definitive, indelible. Eventually, the program resembled a hexagram from the *I Ching.* I'm sure the winner's name had emerged from its unwavering boldness. My own approach is much less precise. What I hope to find is a horse who straddles the line between docility and wildness. Animals ready to compete give off sparks—you can feel a fire building in them. They walk the paddock in tight circles, their energy barely contained. When they stride onto the racing strip, they do so in a confrontational manner, nudging at the outriders' ponies with their noses, or sticking their heads forward in a gesture that smacks of teasing. More than anything, they convey a joy at being alive—it *shines* through. But joy isn't enough if the horse (like Fitch Mountain) belongs with cheaper company. Mr. B.F. did not belong with cheaper company, and he shone like a beacon. I bet him fifty to win, at odds of six to one. He broke first and never bothered to look back.

Suddenly, I had five hundred dollars in my pocket. The bills came in several denominations. They were as crisp as counterfeits, virtually untouched by human hands. They produced such heady oblivion in me that I seemed to be floating through the grandstand on angel wings. My old pal Arnold Walker, who's permanently estranged from Lady Luck, had to bellow my name three times before I descended from the ozone to greet him.

"Did somebody give you nitrous oxide?" Arnold asked, flashing the syrupy, self-effacing grin that causes palpitations of the heart in avid matrons. "Do you want a Valium from the nurse's office?"

I showed Arnold my money.

"Very new," he said.

Bills like those I'd showed him had slipped through Arnold's fingers many times over. He and currency were in a state of perpetual divorce. It was a wonder that he could still afford the expensive suits he liked. The one he had on was beige, with fine pinstripes. He'd bought it during his annual winter trip to Florida, where he visits thoroughbred shrines like Gulfstream Park.

"How'd you do this year?" I asked.

"Terrific," Arnold said dryly. "I broke even."

We had a quick drink at the clubhouse bar, and I tipped the bartender a dollar. Arnold was so startled (he'd never seen me surrender more than fifty cents before) that he launched into a story about a TV ingenue he'd met at a bar somewhere near Boca Raton. He took out his wallet and handed me the matchbook—Rick's Tropical Hideaway— on which she'd scribbled her phone number. "I have it memorized," he said. I cut him short when he began to describe the inside of her condo (pink conch shells, pink satin sheets), and forced him to listen as I used my newfound expertise to tout him on a fourth-race selection.

"Here's an opportunity you won't want to miss," I said. "Check out this Lulugal, Arnold. She's in town from Los Angeles *expressly* to break her maiden. Look who's been handling her at Santa Anita—ace jocks like Shoemaker, McCarron, and Fernando Toro. This is not your ordinary trashy filly. Look at her works." I tapped the small type with my pencil. "Is she in shape? Or is she in shape? Her owner even shipped her up here early, so she could get a feel for the track surface." I paused for effect. "Arnold, I'm giving you this filly like a gift."

Arnold stirred his vodka-and-7-Up. Then he shook his

head sadly. "I'm through with shippers," he said. "I dropped a bundle on some crazy Santa Anita horse in the first."

"The one who was climbing the ladder?"

"You got it."

"But Lulugal's different."

"They're all different when you're in love," Arnold said, hitching up his trousers. "Me, I'm sticking with Plus Ultra. She's steady as a brick."

Why I should have credited the opinion of somebody whose talent as a handicapper is even more suspect than mine, I don't know, but I did credit it, and went for a gloomy stroll around the grounds. Pretty soon, I was riding the escalators, up and down, up and down. I tend to do this when I'm confused, on the assumption that I'll achieve clarity more quickly if I don't have to worry about moving my legs. The escalators failed me, though—I kept getting glimpses of the tote-board. Plus Ultra was an almost even-money favorite, while Lulugal hovered in the risky vicinity of four to one. It did no good to remember that the public was right only a third of the time—*vide* Al Who. The sheer weight of contradictory testimony inhibited me. I was certain Lulugal would win, but I wanted to talk myself out of it.

I wouldn't have played her at all, in fact, if I hadn't had a brief conversation with a man who was also riding the escalators. Actually, he may not have been a man. He had an ethereal quality that linked him to the spirit realm. His hair flew upward in electrified fashion, and his eyes were as scenic as sunsets. He was eating popcorn. He peered over my shoulder and saw "Lulugal" written on the margin of my program, where I'd lovingly inscribed it. "It's Lulugal for sure," the man said pleasantly. "It's got to be Lulugal. I'm telling you, friend, it can *only* be Lulugal." He came closer. "Here's a secret," he said, looking around for G-men in disguise. "Lulugal will win." He thought this was a fabulous joke, and laughed out loud. "Don't you understand?" he said. "It's simple—Lulugal is the best horse. The track's busted me before, and the track will bust me again, but it will not bust me *this* afternoon!" A sort of sigh escaped from his lips. "Lulugal. My Lulu*gal!*"

Of course, it *was* Lulugal, although she managed to create more suspense than I felt was necessary. Her pace was so lackluster that I had to give her some vocal encouragement. This was a sacrifice for me, because I hate to cheer for the horses I've bet. It's one thing to suffer your disappointment in silence and another to announce it to everybody around you. "Lulugal," I muttered. Immediately, a female railbird down the way responded with "Come on, Lulugal!" Her voice had such unthrottled resonance that it summoned forth a more boisterous "Lulugal" from me. My rib cage expanded to free those full, rich syllables—a decidedly therapeutic moment. Before long, a chorus had formed in my section. "Come on, Lulugal!" was the chorus's most popular refrain, followed by "Three horse, Lulugal!" with my bare-bones "Lulugal" in for the show. As the volume of the cheering increased, it seemed finally to filter down to Lulugal's pricked ears, and she picked up the pace. Her breeding and class became apparent when she shifted into overdrive. She won by a length and a half—margin enough to compound the interest on my bankroll and make me wonder if I should hire a Brink's guard to escort me to the car.

I had a bout of recidivism in the next race, when I went against the objective evidence, which pointed to Vin Du Cru, and bet instead Princess Corinne, yet another shipper from L.A. The Princess ran well, but Vin Du Cru beat her to a pulp. I skipped the sixth race. In the seventh, I was interested in an old-timer, Postmark, who'd taken on some heavyweight horses in the past, but I got a scare when I saw him in the paddock. He was *really* old—the kind of still, solemn animal who attracts more than the average number of flies once he's put out to pasture. His groom didn't even walk him around. Postmark just stood in his stall, wearing a faded blanket and letting his eyelids creep toward his nose. I refused to be fooled by Postmark's behavior—older horses are often lazy in the paddock—and approached the windows feeling pure. Postmark delivered the goods, holding on like a veteran to withstand the charge of King Wako, a young upstart. The win pushed my earnings toward the thousand-dollar level. That was all the excitement I could take in a single day, so I slipped through the clubhouse gate, and was confronted again by the familiar glittering blue expanse of San Francisco Bay. For once, I had no desire to jump in.

An hour later, I was sitting in a neighborhood bar, happily involved with the flickering beer signs. Arnold Walker ambled in and propped himself on the nearest stool. All the robustness of Florida had been drained from his face. He looked ashen, as if he'd wintered in a bear cave. He didn't speak but instead turned his jacket pockets inside out. The pockets held lint, ticket stubs, a tube of lipstick, and a broken crayon. So I paid for his vodka-and-7-Up——a double.

"Arnold," I said, adopting the patronizing tone of an older brother, "you'll get over it."

"Tell me about it," Arnold said.

Somebody played "Whiskey River" on the jukebox. Arnold lifted his glass in salute. He hadn't smiled since coming in.

"How much?" I asked.

"Enough to send an underprivileged kid to camp."

In an effort to buoy him up, I told him how well I'd done. I told him how I'd avoided the usual mistakes, and how I'd trusted what was there before my eyes. I told him it was silly to overcomplicate the transparently simple. "You can't let yourself get tangled in the veils, Arnold," I said. "The world is what it is."

Now he smiled. It was a big smile, too, devoid of malice. "Phone me tomorrow," Arnold said. "I want to see if you still believe it in the morning."

J. D. Ross's Vision

The country along the upper Skagit River, in Washington, is hard country. It occupies unfriendly ground. The Cascade Mountains bound it on the east, so that when a wind blows down from Canada, as it often does, it picks up a flinty meanness from all that granite and arrives with such stinging intensity that it echoes between the disks of your spine. A west wind is not much better, since it brings with it mist and chill off the Pacific. The climate throughout the Skagit is wet and cold for most of the year, with heavy snow at the higher elevations. The river valley is fertile, enriched with volcanic ash from Mt. Baker and several feet of topsoil, but corporate farmers prefer to do business on the other side of the Cascades, where they can earn a guaranteed government subsidy just by pumping irrigation water into the desert dust. The upper Skagit is for cranks, romantics, outlaws, and hard cases. It takes a kind of displaced cowboy sensibility to survive, a belief in the terrifying American myth of independence.

The Skagit River is at the heart of things. It originates at a lake in a remote part of British Columbia, then rolls out of the mountains and through the flatlands until it empties into

Puget Sound. The towns on the Skagit are desolate, cut loose from their links to productivity. There was once a thriving concrete industry in Concrete, but the factories are shut down now, hemmed in by neat little company bungalows. In Sedro Woolley, the bars are full of unemployed loggers who drink bottles of Oly and wonder aloud when the hell the machine's going to kick back into gear. Evidence that the machine has faltered is all around them. It shows up in missed house payments, in stacks of unsold goods on market shelves, in the slow, defeated strides of midday strollers on main streets. Even the fishery is in decline. There was a time when the most lackluster poacher could stock his freezer in an afternoon's fishing, but that was a while ago, before any dams had taken a toll.

The dam is a central fact of life in the Pacific Northwest, where a constantly replenished knot of inland waterways once seemed to promise an inexhaustible supply of hydroelectric power. The Columbia River forms the model for what eventually happened to most free-flowing streams in the region——they would be dammed, over and over again, until almost every last ounce of juice had been squeezed out of them. The Columbia is a much larger river than the Skagit, with a flow of 1.9 million gallons of water per second——fourteen times greater than that of the Colorado, which feeds the entire Southwest. In its 1,207-mile rush to the sea, it drops 2,650 feet in elevation and that gives it tremendous force——enough to create one-third of the total hydro capacity of the United States. There are more than twenty multipurpose dams on the Columbia and its tributaries. The most famous are Grand Coulee——as high as a

forty-six-story building and as wide as twelve city blocks—
and Bonneville, in Oregon, about fifty miles east of Portland. In the early 1940s, these dams were producing so
much energy between them that they could have satisfied
the needs of Manhattan, Chicago, Philadelphia, Detroit, Los
Angeles, and Cleveland, but that's not true anymore.

On the Skagit, there are four dams. They were all built
between 1920 and 1940, and they all belong to Seattle City
Light—at present, it is the nation's fifth largest publicly
owned electrical utility. Taken together, the dams constitute
a monument to the man who conceived them, James Del-
mage Ross. In a sense, it was Ross's vision of the upper
Skagit as Hydro Paradise that—along with timber, salmon,
and gold—helped to transform Seattle from a nineteenth-
century port into a complex twentieth-century city.

Born in Chatham, Ontario, in 1872, the son of a Scottish
nurseryman, Ross showed an early predilection for electrical things. At the age of eleven, he made his first battery by
cutting a zinc strip from the apron under his mother's
kitchen stove and combining it with the bottom of an old
copper kettle and some vinegar from a pickle jar. He used
similar batteries to build an electromagnet, and, later, a dy-
namo to light a shop in which he performed scientific experiments. These experiments could be cruel. Ross thought
cats were worthless creatures, because they killed birds, and
he liked to attach wires to a saucer of milk and shock any
poor kitty who stopped for a drink. He had nothing against
dogs, though, and even saved the life of a doomed mongrel,
Sancho, who was about to be destroyed for sucking eggs—

apparently, a grave offense in Chatham. Ross stuck a wired pin in an egg and set it out as bait. When Sancho pounced on it, Ross hit him with a heady jolt, curing the dog of his bad habit. Presumably, he could have hypnotized Sancho just as easily, for he was a student of Mesmer's theories and often put his classmates into trances, then ordered them to do things like declaim "Old Mother Hubbard" while standing on the teacher's desk.

As a young man, Ross contracted tuberculosis. In spite of the disease, he went on a gold-prospecting expedition into the Northwest wilderness, in 1898. He found some gold, and, miraculously, his lungs healed. After returning briefly to Ontario, he left for the Pacific Coast, and in Anacortes, Washington, he got a job as a steam engineer at a salmon-packing plant. He joined Seattle City Light shortly after the company was formed, in 1902, and he was involved in the construction of its first project, a small hydro dam on the Cedar River. In 1911, Mayor George Dilling appointed Ross the new superintendent of City Light. Immediately, Ross started planning to tap the latent energy of the Skagit River.

At the time, the Skagit flowed unhampered all along its length. Every winter, it flooded its banks and damaged crops in a downstream valley known as Skagit Flats. Because of the annual floods, there was tremendous popular support for controlling the river. Around 1905, the Skagit Power Company, based in Denver, posted notices that stated an intent to build several dams at sites in and around Diablo Canyon, a steep-sided cleft in the Cascades, about thirty miles from the Flats. But Skagit Power was short on cash and never made good on its claims. A few years later, Stone & Webster, a Boston firm, acquired Skagit Power and took a more formal approach to development by obtaining legal permits from the Department of Agriculture, locking up the canyon sites through January 1917.

It seemed that Ross would never get a shot at the river, but Stone & Webster, like Skagit Power, failed to deliver. When the firm's permits expired, Ross filed an application on behalf of City Light. In it, he said that he wanted to build two hydro plants—one in Diablo Canyon, and one at Ruby Creek, to the northeast. Actually, he had it in mind to put three dams on the Skagit, the third of them (it was the first to be built) at Gorge Creek, southeast of Diablo. According to Ross, each dam would have a powerhouse. Transmission lines mounted to wooden poles would carry the juice to the city—1.25 million horsepower when the project was done. He might as well have been speaking in terms of cubits. There is something grand and biblical—something virginal—in his calculations.

Secretary of Agriculture David Houston awarded Ross his permit on December 22, 1917. By 1921, a thousand City Light employees were living on the Skagit in rustic cottages and bunkhouses that constituted the construction camp of Newhalem. They had a school, and a volunteer preacher from the Bellingham, Washington, presbytery, and a mini-dam on Newhalem Creek to supply the bosses with electricity. Progress on the Gorge plant was slow, because of the harsh winter weather. The powerhouse—it looks like the Lincoln Memorial—was finished in 1923, but it didn't go into service until the dam was completed more than a

year later. Ross, ever conscious of ceremony, had a gold telegraph key installed at the White House. When President
Calvin Coolidge pressed it, a spark went through the cables
of the Postal Telegraph Cable Company, and Seattle experienced a shock as heady as the one Ross had given to Sancho.

In 1928, Ross escorted twenty-seven members of the
Seattle City Women's Club on a tour of the project. This
outing was the prototype of a more elaborate tour, which by
the mid-1930s was bringing nearly two thousand people a
week to the Skagit during the warm summer months. "We
lure 'em in with a display of beautiful growing things . . ."
Ross said. "When they get here, they see the dam and the
powerhouses—and that's what we want them to see." But it
was the beautiful growing things that made a lasting impres-
sion. Ross turned the project area into an Arabian Nights
fantasy. Exotic flowers and trees were planted by riverside
paths; in winter, the more perishable species, like orchids,
were moved into the Gorge powerhouse to protect them
against frost. At Diablo, Ross collected a menagerie that included pheasants, peacocks, mountain sheep, cockatiels,
African lovebirds, and an albino deer. His masterpiece was
the waterfall at Ladder Creek. There, after dark, visitors
gathered to watch colored floodlights illuminate the cataract
while one of Ross's favorite songs—either "By the Waters
of Minnetonka," or "Hark! Hark! My Soul!"—soared into
the alpine atmosphere.

The plant in Diablo Canyon went into service in 1936,
but Ross did not live to see his cherished Ruby Dam erected.
He died in March 1939, and was buried in a crypt at the

base of Goodell Mountain—renamed Ross Mountain, even as Ruby Dam became Ross Dam and the impoundment behind it Ross Lake—surrounded by flowering Japanese cherry trees that Franklin Delano Roosevelt had dispatched from Washington, D.C., in sympathy.

The system that Ross pioneered gave Seattle the lowest electrical rates in the country for many years. Even today, the Skagit project remains at the core of the City Light operation, but it no longer meets the needs of its customers. The utility began to suffer shortfalls in its generating capacity in the early 1960s, and, to compensate, started buying power from outside sources—primarily from the Bonneville Power Administration, on the Columbia. By the late 1970s, the B.P.A. was having its own problems of "insufficiency" and informed City Light that it would not be able to make up for Seattle's electrical deficits after 1983. Moreover, the price that City Light had to pay for purchased power kept going up, putting the utility in the disadvantageous (if familiar) position of trying to pass on higher costs to its customers. The customers were not happy.

An air of muted panic had set in at City Light. The strategy its planners had devised to carry Seattle into the future had been a failure of some magnitude, because it banked everything on the mighty atom. The Hydro-Thermal Program, it was called. It involved the construction of a network of nuclear power plants—state of the art, as big as any in existence—but it never got off the ground. Almost from its inception, the program was poorly managed, plagued by safety problems, steadily rising interest rates, and resistance from the public. By the time it was finally scrapped, it had cost the utility $25 billion without producing a single unit of electricity.

II

Some forty-odd years after J. D. Ross's death, I got an invitation to join a special tour of the Skagit project and see for myself what the master builder had wrought. The invitation came from an admirer of Ross's, Bob Royer, who is one of Seattle's two deputy mayors. Royer is an old friend of mine. He'd been appointed to his position by his older brother, Charles, whose campaign for Mayor of Seattle he had successfully managed. Now Bob was the administration's expert in energy matters. It was part of his job to act as liaison between the Mayor and City Light. He'd visited the upper Skagit many times during the past few months, talking to City Light employees about a new plan the utility had to solve its problem. The plan had nothing to do with atoms or breeder reactors. Instead, it would exploit the very margins of Ross's vision. City Light wanted to put yet another dam on the river. The proposed dam, known as Copper Creek, would blockade the Skagit about ten miles south of Gorge Dam. It had several drawbacks, Royer said——in his unique vocabulary, it was "negatory"——all of which would become apparent to me once we were on the road.

We drove north from Seattle on a wet, gray winter afternoon. Gradually, the city and its suburbs dropped away behind us, and the landscape began to change. There were truck farms and dairies, acres of open space. Royer loosened his tie, trying to relax. He was in what he described as a "stressed condition"—tired from long hours at the office and suffering from an exacerbated case of premarital heebie-jeebies. He was about to marry Jennifer James, a cultural anthropologist who conducts a popular radio call-in show in Seattle, and he wasn't looking forward to the ceremonial aspects of the undertaking—Anglican retainers, aunts and uncles from dusty corners of the globe, and the inevitable through-the-keyhole reporting of the local press. In order to calm him down, I suggested we stop for drinks at Jo-D's, a loggers' tavern in the middle of nowhere. The place was packed with raw, bearded faces blooming from flannel shirts. Royer hammered the pinball machine, extracting a minimal number of points, and admired an oversized Rainier beer bottle-cap mounted like a hunting trophy on a tavern wall. "That's a nice little facility," he said outside, lighting a Tiparillo. The car filled with stag-party fumes. We set off again, climbing toward the Cascades. Thick stands of Douglas fir appeared in the distance, green spires against a darkening sky.

Near Concrete, a hundred miles from Seattle, Royer grabbed a pair of binoculars from the backseat and fiddled with the focusing mechanism. He scanned the horizon, looking for bald eagles. The birds winter on the river in great numbers. The Skagit was visible off to the right. It was low and emerald-colored, because the weather had been mild, with no major storms since December.

I asked Royer if anybody was fishing. He shook his head. I'd figured as much. The water was too clear. Anglers know that salmon and steelhead are more likely to be fooled by bait or lures if there's a slight camouflage of silt in the water. The Skagit holds five kinds of salmon in season—pink, chum, coho, sockeye, and Chinook. The chum have the most bearing on the lives of the bald eagles. Silvery and with rather distinct markings, chum range in size from eight to eighteen pounds. They begin their Skagit spawning run in late fall. After spawning, they die, and their carcasses drift downstream and wash up on gravel bars in shallow water. That's what attracts the eagles. They consume all the dead fish and then proceed to their breeding territories, probably on the Olympic Peninsula and in the San Juan Islands, Canada, and Alaska. The eagles tend to concentrate in a twenty-seven-mile stretch east of Concrete, between Rockport and Newhalem, because it offers them superior habitat—lots of gravel bars and also good perch sites.

In Marblemount, about midway between Rockport and Newhalem, Royer shouted, "Hey, pull over! Pull *over!*" Before I could shut off the ignition, he'd bolted from his seat and dashed across the road, oblivious of traffic. He stood on a bluff above the Skagit with the binocs glued to his eyes. "There's an eagle in that tree," he said, nodding toward a lightning-blasted fir.

I doubted it. Royer had broken his glasses a few months earlier and had still not replaced them. He operated more or less on automatic pilot. I took the binocs from him and checked the tree. "I think it's a crow, Bob," I said.

Royer shrugged. "You could be right," he said.

The bird flew off, cawing, into deeper woods.

· · · ·

Royer's mistake didn't surprise me. It was exactly the sort that I'd come to expect from him—an enthusiastic mistake, a mistake of the heart. He is a passionate, opinionated man, blessed with a sense of humor about himself. At the moment, though, he looked beat. His job was draining him dry. He had several major administrative headaches, and Copper Creek was one of them. The dam was very controversial. If it was built, it would imperil the survival of the Skagit's eagles by flooding a stretch of river in which thousands and thousands of salmon spawn: above the site, the perpetually high water could prevent any carcasses from washing up on gravel bars; the eagles' food supply would be severely cut. The birds are highly mobile, but it's questionable whether they could find new habitat on the Skagit or any other river of the Pacific Northwest. There just isn't enough food for them. Furthermore, a diminished food supply has a demonstrable effect on breeding—hungry eagles lay fewer eggs. The average eagle's nest contains only two or three delicate specimens, with shells thinned by DDT, so even the most minuscule change in the environment can jeopardize the future of the species.

I stopped at a market on the outskirts of Marblemount so we could stretch our legs. It was the kind of market that gets so little business in winter that the owner would rather talk to you than sell you something, and he was crestfallen when we just bought a couple of Budweisers and left. We sat on a bench in the parking lot—the drizzle that had accompanied us all the way from Seattle had let up—and watched the Skagit roll by.

Royer took the opportunity to tell me about another seri-

ous objection to Copper Creek—more serious, in fact, than
any environmental objections. It had to do with Indian fishing rights. According to an old document (the Point Elliot
Treaty), three tribes (the Swinomish, the Upper Skagit, and
the Sauk-Suiattle) are entitled to fish at their accustomed
grounds on the Skagit, taking salmon and steelhead for sub-
sistence and for commercial gain. Their right was affirmed
in 1974, in a controversial federal court decision known as
Boldt I, *United States* v. *Washington*. Judge Boldt stated in
his decision that a treaty phrase—"in common"—should
be interpreted to mean that fishery resources in Washington
are to be shared equally between Indians and others. If City
Light went ahead with its Copper Creek plan, thereby elimi-
nating part of the annual salmon and steelhead runs, the
Point Elliot tribes would almost certainly sue for reparations. The reparations would be costly.

I wanted to know how much difference Copper Creek
would make in City Light's hydro capacity.

"Three and a half per cent," Royer said glumly. "And
that's not until they get the bastard finished."

"When would that be?"

"Maybe 1990, if nothing goes wrong."

In Royer's opinion, the plan should have been canned
long ago, but it wasn't up to him to decide such things. It
was up to the Mayor and the Seattle City Council, much as it
had been in Ross's day.

"If the plan's so full of holes," I asked, "why all the fuss
with the drift trip?"

"Politics," Royer said. "If Charlie does decide to flood
out those birds, at least he'll know what they look like up
close."

. . .

Around dusk, still without sighting a bald eagle, we reached Newhalem. I recognized it from photos I'd seen of the original construction camp. It hadn't changed very much. It resembled every other company town I've ever been to—rather bland and ordinary—except for its setting, right on the river, and plumb against the base of the Cascades. The mountains lend a sense of fragility to the town. It seems about to be crushed. Several modest frame houses are lined up in barracks formation along the Skagit. Near them, there's a large neon SHERIFF sign, which struck me as incongruous. I thought you'd have to try very hard to pull off a crime in Newhalem. The absolute historical weight of the place mitigated against the possibility of outrage. It's the sort of town where the tiniest infidelity gets poured like cream into the morning coffee.

We drove by the company store and continued along a winding, rock-strewn road that led us past Gorge Dam to Diablo Canyon, five miles away. I parked on a promontory, and we got out to take in the view. The air was wet and heavy again—that palpitant skin of mist so common during Northwest winters. The light was a variegated green, drawing sustenance from the firs on the mountainside and from the river below them. When I walked to the edge of the promontory and stared into the canyon, I was filled with wonder. I seemed to acquire the sudden insignificance of the miniature, frock-coated sojourners you find posed on promontories in the canvases of nineteenth-century landscape paintings. The dwarfing effect of big-time nature accounted for part of my awe, but I was just as moved by Diablo Dam—a curved arc of concrete 380 feet high and 1,180 feet long. I'd never been impressed by a dam before. Most of the ones built during my life have been meant to hurry a land grab or provide water for corporate farmers. But there was something pristine about Diablo—a rightness, I guess. The interplay of aesthetic and engineering values was really a marvel. It was hard to believe that Ross had stood where I had stood and had imagined it. Maybe the quality of the American imagination was grander in those days, stoked by a perception of the country as an undiminished, ever-fructifying resource.

III

It's impossible to spend any time in Newhalem without being touched by Ross's ghost. It hovers over the town, an ectoplasm of no mean proportions. I could feel it when we walked into the Superintendent's House, a dark old two-story place in which we were to be quartered. I half expected Ross to leap out from an alcove, thrumming his fingers against the buttons of his vest, but it was Charles Royer—known as Charlie to almost everybody—who greeted us. Dressed in a flannel shirt, jeans that somebody had ironed, and polished cowboy boots, Charlie looked like an advertising agency's idea of a modern range rider.

I'd met the Mayor before we'd left Seattle. He's forty-two—four years older than Bob—a handsome man who's concerned about his appearance. He has none of Bob's intensity, and only a bit of his boyishness. Charlie's face has a vaguely Indian cast—dark eyes, dark hair, high cheek-

bones. When he speaks, he does so softly and with delibera-
tion, causing listeners to lean forward in a posture of intimacy. His background is in television journalism. Before going into politics, he was the news analyst, or com-
mentator, at KING-TV; Bob was there, too, working as an
on-camera reporter. Charlie campaigned as an honest,
down-to-earth guy, eager to preserve the integrity of Seattle's diverse neighborhoods. His approach was decidedly lib-
eral, but his administration so far had been more of a
middle-of-the-road affair. Still, he remained a popular figure, very active in the Democratic party. Nobody knew exactly how ambitious he was, but there was suspicion in some
quarters that he would someday make a strong bid for gov-
ernor.

In Seattle, Charlie had been friendly and open, but now
he seemed withdrawn and preoccupied, even a little nervous. Bob had told me that his brother wasn't happy about
the trip or Copper Creek in general. The Mayor had inherited a lame-duck superintendent, with whom he'd had
disagreements, and his own appointee had not worked out
as he had hoped. At present, the job was vacant, and the bureaucrats at the utility were anxious about it. They were
used to taking their cues from a leader—any leader,
really—and they weren't certain anymore if they were toe-
ing the party line.

I ate dinner with the Mayor and his staff at the aptly
named Gorge Inn. It had beanery tables and chairs. There
was a photo of Ross on one wall. He looked like an owl, with
squinty little eyes behind thick spectacles. Ordinarily, the
Gorge is only open in summer, to feed fried chicken and

canned spaghetti to the tourists who still stream in from the city to witness the Skagit's miracles, but we were treated to a more elaborate spread. Poached salmon, asparagus hollandaise, apple pies, pitchers of buttermilk—the meal recalled Ross's unconstricted era. It was designed to knock the stays out of corsets, to keep a logger working for ten hours straight. I saw just one trencherman at the tables who was sizable enough to do justice to the feast. Our bodies had gotten pared down since the 1920s, along with our expectations.

A town meeting had been scheduled for that evening, so that the Skagit workers could meet the Mayor and tell him what they thought about Copper Creek. It was held at Currier Hall, right across from the Gorge. Around fifty people live in Newhalem, and thirty more upriver in Diablo, and most of them showed up—there wasn't much else to do on a Skagit Friday night. The men had ruddy outdoor faces and military haircuts. The women were demure and styleless, and they kept mostly to themselves, chatting about domestic things.

The lives that Skagit families choose to lead seem odd to an outsider. Newhalemites pride themselves on being able to transcend adversity. They tell stories—or folktales, actually—about particularly rough winters, about blizzards and avalanches that block roads for days on end. Fresh milk becomes a luxury item in such circumstances, and dinners are served up out of the deep freeze. Telephone wires are constantly falling down or shorting out, cutting off contact with civilization. You'd think that in this pioneering atmosphere, families would gather together around the hearth and maybe read aloud to one another, but they don't. They try to watch TV—"Little House on the Prairie," reruns of "The Waltons." Reception is usually terrible, because the town's primary antenna sits five thousand feet up a mountain and keeps blowing over.

About eight o'clock, the Mayor walked to the front of the hall and gave a short, unenthusiastic speech. He didn't mention Copper Creek at all, and so confirmed a suspicion among City Light employees that he was not in favor of the dam. Afterward, I talked to some workers, and they were forthright and unanimous in their complaints. They felt that the Mayor was being dodgy, playing coy, and that their labors would be wasted if Copper Creek got scuttled. They interpreted resistance to the project as an affront to their function in society, which was to build. They longed for a Rossian Eden—a place with no bureaucrats or red tape. As they collared Royer to extol Copper Creek's virtues, they seemed blind to the complex texture of the enterprise. They were decent, earnest, and exceedingly loyal—marines on the beachhead of energy—but they were helpless when confronted with a situation that could not simply be subdued.

"Politics," one man said, heading for the door.

The tour proper began in the morning. Darci Covington, a young woman from City Light's community relations department, joined us after we'd eaten a truly monstrous breakfast at the Gorge Inn. She had the tour guide's implacable efficiency and moved us along at a brisk pace—

which was not unwelcome, because it was cold. The temperature hovered near thirty-eight degrees, but an icy wind cutting through the canyon increased the chill factor substantially.

We drove in a convoy to the Diablo plant. The dam looked even more monumental than it had when I saw it from the promontory. We stopped at the Tour Center Museum, where Ross's rolltop desk is on exhibit, along with his spectacles, an electric range he sold to City Light customers, and a faded copy of a book he wrote on physics—*New Views of Space, Matter, and Time.* Then we entered the Diablo powerhouse. It was like walking into a submarine; the natural world dropped away. I was aware of a slight humming noise, like a bee buzzing in a vacuum. Everything was dustless, spit-clean. Men in hard hats padded by, treading softly on crepe-soled shoes, as if they were afraid to disturb the sanctity of the place. The two main generators—cylindrical, flat on top—were in a cavernous white-walled room at the back of the powerhouse. Painted a pastel shade of peach, they had a hi-tech beauty. A little iron plaque was attached to each of them: S. MORGAN SMITH CO. PENNSYLVANIA U.S.A. Here was the Machine Age in apotheosis, a silent homage to invention. In their splendid isolation, the generators seemed so self-contained that it was difficult to remember that they depended on the river for their power—on unpredictable accumulations of rain and snow.

From the powerhouse, we went to a boat landing nearby and boarded the *Cascadian,* a diesel-engined ferry that carried us across Diablo Lake, to Ross Dam. The dam extends five hundred and forty feet from river bedrock to the road

that runs along its crest. Some of us climbed stairs inside the
dam to get to the road. The stairs had been used during the
dam's construction. Workers had carted up bags of cement,
loads of lumber, sacks of tools, but we had trouble just willing our bodies forward. Water dripped onto our heads,
steady as a pulse. It dripped down the interior walls, too, and
had leached calcium deposits from the rock. The deposits
glistened, like stalactites in a cave.

Finally, I burst through the door at the top of the stairs,
glad to have made it. Bob Royer followed me. He was bent
double, sucking in air. "I don't really think I enjoyed that,"
he said.

Together, we strolled along the crest road. The wind
gusted up from the river; a fine powder of snow blew into
our faces. To the north, the Cascades swept toward the sky.
They resembled the Swiss Alps—pristine, unvanquished.
"Hey, check this out," Royer said. He showed me a
plaque—larger than the ones on the generators—set into
the wall of the dam. It informed us that an urn containing
the ashes of Glen Harry Smith, an assistant superintendent
who died in 1939, had been interred in Section 12, midway
between Contraction Joints 11 and 12, fifty feet from the
face of the dam. A quotation from First Corinthians was inscribed on the plaque:

> According to the grace of God which is
> given unto me, as a wise masterbuilder,
> I have laid the foundation, and another
> buildeth thereon. But let every man take
> heed how he buildeth thereupon.

Suddenly, a bald eagle took flight from a mountain crag
some five hundred yards away, soaring upward, its wings

spread wide. Some ethologists think that bald eagles fly only out of necessity, to hunt or scavenge, but others say that the birds sometimes choose to soar for no apparent reason. This seemed to be true of the bird we were watching. The eagle was just riding the wind, two thousand feet above the river and wheeling higher and higher. Bald eagles have an acute ability to locate thermals—rising bodies of warm air—even on still days. When the wind is blowing, it's a gift to them. They can cover vast territories in an effortless way, searching for food. If necessary, they'll stoop to kill live prey or pirate a fish from a hawk, but they'd as soon feed on carrion. Such ignoble behavior prompted Benjamin Franklin to object to the bald eagle's presence on the national seal. "He is a bird of bad moral character," Franklin wrote in a letter to his daughter. "He does not get his living honestly." The wild turkey would have been a better selection, Franklin thought—more likely to "attack a grenadier of the British Guards should the soldier invade his farmyard with a red coat on."

Returning to Diablo on the *Cascadian,* my collar turned up against the cold, I talked with R. J. Stretch, a crew-cut man in his fifties who has a vehement exactitude about him. The pens and pencils in his shirt pocket were arranged in precise order; you got the feeling that he knew even before he went to bed what he'd wear in the morning. Stretch is responsible for overseeing the entire Skagit project, making certain that everything is fine-tuned. He grew up in Montana, and he told me what it's like to hike into the mountains in autumn hoping to pack out enough deer or elk meat to supply a family through the winter. Stretch was typical of Newhalemites in that he wanted to build Copper Creek. He wanted to build nuclear plants, too; he played down the hazards. "You'll have accidents," he said. "You can't avoid them." Stretch knew of a town where there were traces of uranium in the drinking water. "It doesn't hurt anybody," he said.

The float trip down the Skagit was anticlimactic. It started after lunch. Our party had increased in size, thanks to the appearance of Congressman Al Swift, of Bellingham—a Copper Creek opponent—who had an entourage of aides and reporters. The reporters cornered Charlie Royer and pressed him on the issues. He answered the questions snappishly, giving no indication of his true feelings. The Mayor did not seem to be enjoying the great outdoors or the publicity aspects of the trip. He'd stayed close to his bodyguard for most of the morning, looking tight-lipped and reserved. Now, between answers, he was blowing on his hands. The cold had him bouncing up and down on his feet. "I'm a city boy," he said, smiling.

We left from Goodell Creek, just south of Newhalem. There were nine rubber rafts, each with a scruffy river rat at the helm. They divided us among the rafts, distributing the weight as evenly as possible. The Skagit was still low. The current lacked thrust. Our boatman, a bearded, barrel-chested kid in red suspenders, had to push hard on the oars to keep us from idling. The sky was dull and gray.

It was a nine-mile float to Copper Creek. It took four hours. The thrills were few and far between. Halfway through, we did tear into a canyon S curve riddled with boulders and small rapids, but they were run without any trouble and gave us less of a charge than climbing the stairs at Ross Dam had done. The rafts bent in half and took on water. Voyagers in slickers and rain suits managed fine, but those of us in sneakers and old peacoats felt an awful clamminess descend.

We saw about twenty bald eagles along the route. They were perched high in the limbs of firs and alders. None of them were actively feeding. It was the wrong time of day (they feed early and late), and besides, food was in short supply. The last flood, in early December, had washed most chum carcasses downstream. I'd read that bald eagles are spooked by human beings, but these birds didn't move when we drifted past. They had marvelous balance. Their austere white heads looked fierce through the binoculars. There was a sleekness in them that's missing in other scavengers. Vultures don't touch the heart. When eagles take off, they seem noble somehow, in tune with the innocent ideals of the republic.

No sign marked the Copper Creek site. Our boatman had to point it out as we floated by. I tried to imagine what the finished project would look like: an earth-and-rock-fill dam, to be built on river deposits instead of bedrock, so that the structure could shift with the shifting subsoil; a powerhouse, spillway, and switchyard; a reservoir, ten miles long, reaching all the way back to Gorge powerhouse and flattening out the rapids we'd just run. The project would devour two thousand three hundred acres of land. Deer, bears, beavers, small mammals, reptiles, amphibians, and birds would die. Ten miles of state highway would have to be relocated, along with up to ten miles of transmission lines. All this for a marginal dose of power.

We beached the rafts at Bacon Creek. The sky broke, and a light rain fell. Bob Royer and I were drenched to the skin. We got a ride back to Newhalem with R. J. Stretch. Stretch had not rafted the river, but he'd followed our progress from the highway, picking up empty beer cans along the road. The cans covered the floor of his car. Each of them had been stomped upon, crushed as flat as a quarter. Stretch dropped us at the Superintendent's House. We changed into dry clothes and packed our bags for Seattle. There was a frenzy about our departure, almost an aspect of escape. The past seemed about to swallow us, foreclosing on the future.

IV

Once we were back in Seattle, and somewhat recuperated, the Skagit tour began to seem stranger than ever to me, but I didn't find out what Charlie Royer had thought about it until the next afternoon, when we joined him to watch the Super Bowl at the house of Don McGaffin, a crony from KING-TV days. The Mayor was in a good mood, freed from Newhalem's constraints. Some of the Skagit's physical beauty had been lost on him, not because he was impervious to landscape glories but because he was charged with the task of mediating among wildly divergent parties. He was supposed to keep eagles flying, salmon spawning, rapids crashing, and light bulbs burning, all without spending much money. The dilemma at Copper Creek was a hoary one, recapitulating in part the classic late-century encounter between the snail darter and the Tennessee Valley Authority at Tellico Dam, but that didn't make it any easier to write a satisfactory conclusion.

The Mayor said that he, too, had been surprised by the anachronistic character of Newhalem—it had the quality of a time warp. He was most concerned about the welfare of City Light's employees there. He said that it was sad that nobody took them into account in discussions of environmental impact. The Skagit employees had served the utility well for years, and now, because of shifting energy priorities, their view of the world—and of public service—was becoming obsolete. For Charlie Royer, the underlying problem was how to instill the values of Ross's time into a new group of workers. He didn't say what he was going to do about the dam.

That question was answered on Monday. A front-page story appeared in the morning *Post-Intelligencer,* under the headline ROYER AND SWIFT SHOOT RAPIDS AT DAM SITE. As everyone had expected, it made Congressman Swift sound heroic, a champion of the Skagit biota, while the Mayor was portrayed as a conniver. "A young bald eagle perched atop a tree at almost the exact spot where the dam would cross the river," wrote the *P-I*'s reporter, preparing to unleash some anthropomorphic Guignol. "Unlike other eagles, it did not fly away but glared down as Royer's boat floated by."

In the afternoon, the Mayor released to the press City Light's recommendation to him on Copper Creek. The recommendation was signed by Acting Superintendent Joe Miller. It suggested that the utility not file an application for a federal license to build the dam; that all current studies and investigations be terminated at once; and that the project be placed in abeyance for not more than four years.

The Mayor would take this recommendation into account and submit it to the City Council with his own recommendation. I asked Bob Royer what the Mayor's recommendation would be.

"Against construction," he said.

What the Mayor wanted instead was for City Light to invest in a coal-powered plant to be built in Creston by the Washington Water Power Company. Coal was quantifiable, absolute. No drought would ever shut down the Creston plant.

Royer told me that other plans were on the boards at City Light. None of them sounded encouraging.

There was a plan to raise Ross Dam by a hundred feet or so, increasing its generating capacity. There was a plan to put a powerhouse and penstock near an existing dam on the south fork of the Tolt River. There was a plan to build a new dam on the north fork of the Tolt. There was a plan to use sewage. There was a plan to tap into geothermal wells. There was a plan to disperse wind-turbine generators at selected sites around the state. There were several plans for saving energy through conservation.

I ended my stay in Seattle by joining Bob Royer for a dip in his hot tub, which rests on a deck overlooking Lake Washington. We felt like energy criminals, to be using up precious kilowatts for such a frivolous purpose. Across the lake, millions of bulbs were blinking away, fueled, perhaps, by power from the Skagit—the miraculous transformation

of water into light. How many other miracles of transformation went unnoticed in cities everywhere? I watched Royer
sink chin-deep in the tub. He was still anxious about his
wedding, and a little depressed about Copper Creek. He
talked about leaving politics to take a job in the private sec-
tor. Then he talked about writing a suspense novel—some
thickly plotted trifle geared to earning him a million bucks.

As I bobbed around, I wondered what Ross would have
thought of hot tubs. Probably, he would have liked them. He
had a taste for gadgets. He might have figured a way to sell a
tub to every customer in Seattle, much as he'd sold ranges
to their grandparents. And I was willing to bet that after he
got the tubs installed, he'd have figured out how to keep the
water hot without pulling too hard on the system. That was
the puzzling thing about City Light's dilemma—the utility
seemed terribly short on new ideas. No doubt the planners
were up against a more difficult situation than Ross had
faced; and yet what they had to offer the public was nowhere
as bold. Maybe the future really was unimaginable. The
American brain seemed compacted—as used up as the
frontier that once had given it wings.

Royer and I agreed that Copper Creek was a stale
project, left over from the 1930s. What City Light needed
was a new vision to carry it forward, for the great lesson of
the Skagit, and of Ross's career, was that a sustaining vision
can itself be a kind of energy.

O'Neill
Among the Weakfish

Eastern Long Island is famous for its saltwater fishing, but when I moved into the summer house I'd rented there, in the woods between Sag Harbor and East Hampton, I discovered that I hadn't brought along the proper tackle. So I went directly to a place I'll call O'Neill's Tackle Shop to stock up. O'Neill himself waited on me. He referred to the rod he sold me as a "stick." The reel, he said, was guaranteed. "It's got gears," he told me, cracking it open, like a walnut. "You want crap, I'll sell you Japanese."

"No thanks," I said.

O'Neill closed one eye, held out the stick, and examined it for bruises. He was pleased with what he saw.

"This is about as good a stick as you're going to get," he said, "for what you're willing to pay."

"What if I paid more?"

"Then you're talking custom sticks." He spat into an ashtray. "You're approaching elegance."

"Forget it," I said.

O'Neill wound the reel with fifteen-pound test line. He sold me some two-ounce weights, some purple plastic worms, and some lead-headed jigs—heavy lures that sink quickly and ride upside-down in the water, making them resistant to snags.

"You'll need squid for bait," he said, reaching into a small refrigerator and grabbing packages. "Skimmer clams. Mussels." He paused for a moment and surveyed the dead and semidead items on the counter. "You ought to have some real worms. You want some real worms?"

"Whatever you say, O'Neill."

"Yeah, you better have some real worms."

The counter was stacked high with smelly stuff. Clam juice leaked out of a Styrofoam tub. O'Neill tipped back his baseball cap and sold me a map that showed all the creeks, ponds, lakes, bays, and ocean beaches in Suffolk County. He sold me a spike-like rod holder to drive into the sand, so I'd always have a hand free for drinking beer. He sold me a fishing license and a bumper sticker that read, *Surf Casters Do It in the Dark*. When I finally said no to a fillet knife, he looked around the shop in a panic. "How about a clam rake? A crab net?"

"No dice."

"This is a terrific folding chair."

"Just the bill," I said.

O'Neill sighed and did some quick addition on a paper napkin. I gave him a credit card, and he spent about ten minutes in search of his machine. He found it in a bottom drawer, in a nest of monofilament.

"Ninety-seven fifty," he said, after he'd filled in the form, painstakingly, writing each number with devout attention to its peculiarities. "Ah, what the hell. Let's call it an even ninety-five. I'll toss in the squid for free."

I asked him where the action was.

"Hang on a second," he said, as he filled in a new form. "Can't you see I'm working here?"

I walked around the shop while he worked. It wasn't a very big place, maybe fifteen by twenty feet, with a pair of glass display cases that took up most of the space. On the walls, there were photos of locals who'd brought in trophy catches for O'Neill to record with his Instamatic—striped bass, bluefish, blackfish, even a shark that somebody had nailed on a party boat that had gone out from Montauk, at the very tip of the Island. I started thinking how tackle shops everywhere are the same, with the same odors of bait and stale tobacco worn into the wood, and the same smiling anglers taped up in all their glory between placards of lures. There's always an overzealous O'Neill behind the counter—some guy who wants to divest himself of as much tackle as possible without falling into outright criminality.

The first tackle shop I remember visiting was in White Bear Lake, Minnesota. I must have been six or seven. I stood at the counter next to my father, who seemed huge, the way every father does to his kid—at least when the kid is young. He was dropping a bundle of money on an assortment of tackle that the clerk—dog-faced, with a pack of Chesterfields rolled up in the sleeve of his T-shirt—assured him was absolutely essential. "Oh, yeah, you got to have a Buzz-Bomb," the clerk was saying. "Nobody around here goes out without a Buzz-Bomb. And the fish have really been socking these Sonics. A Sonic drives the big fish wild." The lures were pretty useless, of course, and ended their lives hooked on branches or lily pads, but I remember how excited my father was to own them. That's how I felt when I grabbed my new stick and began whipping it through the air, startling poor O'Neill.

"So you want to know where the action is?" he asked.

"Sure," I said.

He told me I should get myself all rigged up and go over to Long Beach, on Gardiners Bay. The annual weakfish run was on, and the boys over there were murdering them every night. "And you got everything you need to score," he said.

"I'll bet."

O'Neill squeezed my shoulder. "I'll tell you the truth, kiddo," he said. "I wish'd I could go with you."

The trip to Long Island was in the nature of a homecoming for me. I'd been living in California for years, but I grew up in Westbury, in the Island's central section, back in the days when many of the present suburbs were still potato fields, and you could look down the main drag and see all the way to Manhattan. My father bought our house, a Levitt tract model, for about eight thousand dollars, in 1950. He didn't have to put any money down, since he was a veteran. The house was only a twenty-minute drive from the Atlantic, but he seldom did any saltwater fishing, mainly because he was from the upper Peninsula, in Michigan, and the ocean was always a bit too overwhelming for him to handle. Every summer, he'd get the itch for freshwater, for bass and northern pike, and he'd pack the family into the Country Squire station wagon and off we'd go to Minnesota, where my mother's relatives lived. The idea was to rent a cottage by a lake—White Bear, Paradise, Big Kandiyohi, there were ten thousand of them to choose from. Probably I caught my first fish in Minnesota, but I don't recall anymore what kind it was. It could have been a crappie or a sunfish or even a perch. The rest of the vacation set is fixed in my mind, though, because its details varied so little from year to year.

The cottage, no matter where it was, had a screened porch where the kids got to sleep. In the mesh of the screens, you could find enough bug corpses to construct an archaeology of insect life, dating from the turn of the century. The beds on the porch had lumpy mattresses spotted with mildew. The kitchen in the cottage was always too small. It had a linoleum floor, a fridge that hummed and snorted, and a sticky yellow fly strip dangling from the ceiling. The bathroom door never closed properly—you had to secure it with a piece of wire. When the door was open, it brushed against the edge of the Formica-topped table where the aunts were playing canasta. The table had decals on it—leaping fish, beavers chewing on logs. The aunts tried to move it away from the bathroom door, toward the middle of the kitchen, but the uncles complained that it blocked their path to the beer. They drank beer all day long, cases of it. They had big sunburned Slovenian noses that looked ready to burst. They talked about the Army, about Eisenhower and Jayne Mansfield, and ignored the strange tribe of children known as "the cousins." These cousins (they were nameless entities) had hobbies. They collected rocks and butterflies, and stamps from foreign countries. At night, when the aunts put them to bed in the cottage next door, we could hear them singing camp songs in spooky, high-pitched voices.

I looked forward to these vacations until I hit my thirteenth birthday, and then I rebelled. I wanted to assert my independence, to establish that I had an existence apart from my parents. What good was Minnesota to a teenager? Did they have any rock 'n' roll there? Doubtful—they hardly had any *Negroes*. So what was an intelligent, hard-nosed, rock 'n' roll, Long Island kid like me going to do at a lake? Go *fishing?* The notion was too dumb to credit. Besides, I had obligations. I couldn't afford to miss any Babe Ruth League baseball games, not when my team (Mr. Wong's Chinese Restaurant) was a pennant contender. Furthermore, I had this girl friend, a stacked brunette, who'd let me slip my hand under her sweater while we were watching an Elvis Presley movie at the Meadowbrook, and I thought that by August, if I could keep coming up with the ticket money, she might let me touch her bra. Were there any teenage girls in Minnesota who'd grant me such favors? Don't make me laugh! I didn't put the argument quite so boldly, but I did grovel and whine with such hideous determination that the following summer I was given a choice about the vacation. I chose to stay home.

My father gradually expanded his vacation horizons. He took everybody to upstate New York, to Maine, and once, splurging, to the Canadian wilderness, in pursuit of giant muskies. I never went along. I was too busy with adolescence, with my own face in the mirror. I figured that I'd given up on fishing, but there came a time, soon enough, when drifting aimlessly through the middle of nowhere seemed as fine and peaceful an activity as anybody could hope to engage in.

. . .

The weakfish season on Long Island generally lasts from May to October. The fish tend to run in schools and have a liking for shallow, sandy areas. They feed on a wide range of marine life, so they can be found at different levels in the water. In shoals, they'll rise right up to the surface to prey on baitfish, like killies and minnows. Catching them is a tricky business. They usually strike quickly, with force, and streak off in unpredictable directions—sometimes straight at you, so that you have to gather slack line as fast as you can to keep them from getting away. Most sporting writers remark on their beauty. Weakfish are said to resemble sea trout. Slim and bright, they flash a spectrum of color when they swim by—smudges of green, purple, lavender, gold, blue, all dabbed on a field of sparkling silver. They are prized for their flavor as well as for their beauty. Their flesh is lean and flaky, very delicate, an incandescent white.

I was thinking about a weakfish dinner the first night I drove over to Long Beach, a strip of sand and pebbles that fronts on Gardiners Bay. I got there at dusk, just as the sun was setting. I'd invited my father to join me, but he lived almost fifty miles away, and he was unwilling to commit himself to the quest until I had some practical experience. All along the shore, the boys O'Neill had talked about were casting lures and bait, with an energy that bordered on the obsessional. The boys ranged in age from about sixteen to seventy. Behind them, in a parking lot, they had assembled a fleet of vehicles of a type you see only in the East—rusted-out V-8 sedans that seem nothing so much as the final tortured outcry of the Industrial Revolution.

I put on my hip boots and stood between two boys who

were knee-deep in the surf. I tried some squid first, thread-
ing chucks of it on a pair of hooks that hung below a pyrami-
dal weight—a special weakfish setup—but the squid just sat
on the floor of the bay, unattended to except by thieving
crabs. I switched over to a purple plastic worm trailing from
a lead-headed jig and started casting the way the others
were doing. The worm flew out about fifty yards, then sank
slowly to the bottom. I retrieved it slowly, too, dragging it
inch by subtle inch across clamshells, rocks, and submerged
beer cans, as I'd learned to do while fishing for largemouth
bass in California. This was an interesting exercise in underwater topology, but nothing more, so I changed over to a
minnow-like plug. (Plugs are lures that usually resemble a
small fish.) It brought no takers.

Nobody else on the beach was having any luck. A few of
the boys had jammed their sticks into rod holders, then repaired to their rusting hulks to suck on beers and complain
about the state of the universe, with particular regard to the
shortage of weakfish in Gardiners Bay. I gathered that this
was an integral part of the saltwater game, so I repaired to
my own unrusted Datsun for a drink. A boy called Eddie noticed my California plates and struck up a conversation. He
believed absolutely in the power of squid.

"Why is any fish going to bite a piece of plastic?" he
asked, speaking in the general direction of the sky.
"Wouldn't you rather eat good, fresh squid?"

"I think the idea is to fool them."

"I don't go in for tricks," Eddie said. "Maybe you do,
being from California. Everything's fake out there. The
people. The fish. Everything!"

I was saved from further assault when Eddie leaped to his feet and shouted, "Somebody's got one on!"

We ran down to the shore, where a tall boy in a Mozart sweat shirt was wrestling with a weakie. It was evident from the way his rod was bent that *weakfish* is a misnomer. The name is not intended to characterize the fish's fighting ability. It refers instead to the tender tissue around the fish's mouth; the tissue tears free of a hook at the slightest undue pressure. The tall boy knew this. He coaxed the weakie, reeling it in ever so gently. The fish didn't want to quit. The tide gave it some extra leverage. It made several good runs, working against the tall boy's muscle. Once, the fish made the line sing, and we all murmured in awe. There's an angler's prayer you whisper at such moments: *At least let me see the fish.* Losing a fish you've hooked is bad, but it's infinitely worse to lose one you haven't seen. That's simply too much mystery. Something that's rightfully yours sinks into the realm of the invisible.

When the tall boy beached the weakie at last, there was a shared sense of relief among us, and we moved closer to examine the spoils. The fish lay on a pile of glistening kelp. Its gills were opening and closing rapidly, gasping for air. The tall boy bent down and took out his hook. It came away easily, without any effort. A tentacle of squid was stuck to the fish's mouth, and Eddie nudged me with an elbow.

"You listen to what I been telling you," he said.

I was caught up in the fish's colors—blue, green, and purple along the sides, so brilliant in the moonlight that I had to blink.

"It's only a school fish," Eddie said. "Maybe seven pounds."

"They get much bigger?"

"I've seen 'em come out of here twelve, thirteen pounds."

The fish pushed the boys back into action. I tried squid again, then real worms, then the minnow plug. Down on the beach, I heard shouts that indicated another weakie was on, but after they died down, it was quiet for a long time. Around ten o'clock, the crowd began to thin. Those V-8 engines spewed out clouds of exhaust, adding an overlay of petroleum distillates to the salty atmosphere. I stayed on the beach until midnight. My arms ached from the casting, and my back was sore from the standing. I hadn't got a bite, unless you counted the nibbling of crab pincers, but I was very happy, baptized in a way, and I looked forward to the evening when it would be my fish that started the boys to murmuring. I dumped my bait on a rock, where the gulls would make short work of it. Just as I was leaving, an egret passed overhead, its white wings flapping against the moon.

I returned to Long Beach the next night, and the night after that, but I still had no success, so I checked in with O'Neill to be sure I was using the right techniques. Once again, he made a careful survey of my rod.

"Stick's fine," he said. "Maybe you're getting over there too early."

"No chance."

"Maybe you're not staying late enough."

"No chance."

O'Neill scratched his ear. "Maybe the fish don't like you," he said.

I decided to experiment. It seemed logical to me that if weakfish were not thick around Long Beach, they might be thick somewhere else, cruising the shoreline while they looked for good spawning ground, so I picked a likely bay beach near East Hampton. It was bordered by scrub oaks, dogwood, and a few maples. There were two or three houses hidden in the trees. The bay had a sandy bottom. The average person could wade into it for two hundred yards before the water rose to shoulder level.

I got to the beach early on a gray Sunday afternoon. I had my tackle and bait, a lawn chair, and a copy of the wartime journals of the Greek poet George Seferis. The book was an affectation. I always think that I'm going to sit in a chair or on a rock and read ecstatic literature while I'm waiting for a fish, but it never happens. I look at two words, three words, a sentence, and then some beautiful bird flies by, or a horseshoe crab creeps out of the surf, and I lose my place. Language pales in comparison to the syntax of nature, I guess, which is why Louis Agassiz could write thousands of pages in an attempt to describe the simple jellyfish. Agassiz must have been terribly frustrated when a contemporary, eyeing the creature in question, remarked, "Why, it's little more than organized water!"

The bay tide looked right. It was outgoing, and that meant that small baitfish would be washed to sea toward the weakies—if the weakies were there. Surprising, then, given such perfect circumstances, that no other anglers were around, I saw herring gulls, and some romantic couples strolling along the sand, but my stick was the only one in evidence.

After I made my first cast, I snapped open the lawn chair and sat down. I tried Seferis.

> *In essence,* the poet has one theme:
> his live body.

Minutes later, I was interrupted—not by the usual pantheistic revery, but by the unmistakable sound of Perry Como singing, "Don't Let the Stars Get in Your Eyes." The record was blasting out of one of those secluded houses back in the trees. Perry sang "Don't Let the Stars Get in Your Eyes" five times in the next half hour, at an ever-increasing volume. When Perry wasn't singing, Frankie Laine or Vaughn Monroe was. A musical era that deserves to be forgotten was instead being re-created right there on the beach. I started to mumble harsh judgments against homeowners who destroy fragile ecological balances by introducing lame songs into an aural spectrum that gulls, terns, ospreys, and so on ought to dominate.

I was about to yell something obscene when I noticed that a young woman had left the arm of her partner in romance and was about to take my picture. She had me framed against the bay; I could have been an old salt down from Montauk. My dream of catching a weakfish was suddenly base, reduced to postcard material, no more than local color. That would have been the ultimate tribulation of the afternoon if it hadn't started to rain. I'm talking big rain, your basic cats-and-dogs.

In a drenched, despondent condition, I reported to O'Neill. He gave me coffee and sold me an emergency poncho that folds up to the size of a dime and fits in your trouser pocket.

"You was wasting your time," he said. "Nobody the hell's ever caught a weakie off that beach."

"Why not?"

"Because that's how God made it, is why not."

Another pantheist.

"Anyhow, the fish is more offshore now," O'Neill said. "What you really need is to get yourself a boat."

"I'll bet you sell boats."

O'Neill shrugged. "There's outfits that'll rent you one," he said.

I found a rental outfit in Sag Harbor. I went there with my optimistic father, who brought a landing net, and my brother, who happened to be in town from California. Among us, we'd collected an amazing assortment of tackle, including a tiny boat rod, stiff as a piece of hickory, and a lightweight rod-and-reel that would have been perfect for sunnies at a Minnesota lake.

The skiffs rented for twenty-nine dollars a day, but the guy let us have ours for twenty-five, since it was already past noon—too late, really, to be headng out. "I doubt you'll do much," he said, offering advance consolation. He handed us a map that showed the primary spots frequented by stripers and porgies, as well as weakfish.

My brother thought that my father should pay for the skiff, because it was my father's birthday. Such inverse reasoning is not uncommon in our family, conferring privilege in a backward sort of way.

I don't know how long it had been since we'd all gone out

together in a boat. We took up a lot more space than we had in the past, three men instead of two boys and an adult. There was some jostling for position. I felt the closeness of skin, that familiar intimacy, tempered, as ever, by the need to assert my independence. But the need was much diminished, an advantage of being older.

My brother fired up the outboard, then asked for a beer from the cooler. He wanted to go to the opposite shore—a thirty-minute ride. My father, a nonswimmer, wanted to stay closer to the harbor, on the assumption that he'd have a better chance of being saved if he fell in.

We started for the opposite shore.

My father had a beer. I had a beer.

The water was choppy, but the spray, coming at us, felt good. The sun was hot. I took off my shirt: *the live body*.

When we reached our destination, my brother cut the motor. Our barely articulated plan was to drift from the shore's eastern end to a rocky point at its western tip, through a region marked *weakfish* on the map. I baited a double-hooked O'Neill rig with squid and dropped it over. It hit bottom at about ten feet, so I reeled in some line. I used the same kind of rig on the tiny boat rod. The others tried Salty Dogs—soft plastic lures that shimmer like baitfish underwater.

For a while, we just drifted along, rocking in the big silence that always follows a motor shutting down. The rocking was pleasant, with its complement of sailing gulls, and the salt smell everywhere. It took me back to those summer vacations, and the red-nosed uncles, and the aunts with their playing cards. The sheer and simple grandeur.

It was only right that my father should get the first strike.

He'd paid for the skiff, after all, and he'd just turned sixty-eight. His rod bowed suddenly. The line on his little reel—it couldn't have been more than six-pound test—went ripping out at an alarming rate.

"Check your drag," my brother advised him.

He fumbled with the knob on his reel, loosening it so that the line went out more readily, with less resistance. He couldn't apply much pressure, not with such flimsy gear. This put him under stress, because he's a legendarily impatient angler.

"Keep your rod high," I told him. "Make the fish work."

"I *know* what I'm doing," he said sharply.

The fish took out more line. My father got some back. The dance was a classic one—gain and loss, loss and gain. For twenty minutes, it continued, until the fish got tired, and my father led it slowly to the side of the boat. Again I saw those colors—blue, green, purple—more vibrant than ever in the swirling water.

My brother, handling the net, said, "It's a salmon."

"I don't think so," I said.

It was a weakie—a broad female full of roe. She had a mottling of dark green spots along her back. We put her in the cooler with the beer.

My father was smiling from ear to ear. He looked about twenty-five. The fish was the biggest he'd caught in years.

Almost immediately, the boat rod began hammering against the skiff's gunwales. I grabbed it and set the hook. This fish didn't fight as well. The rod's stiffness was too much for it. I brought the fish to net in less than ten minutes—another weakie, as brilliant as the first, although smaller. I wished that I'd taken it in the surf on my O'Neill rod-and-reel. The odds would have been better. The fish would have had an edge.

When fish strike back-to-back, with unexpected intensity, I always believe that the action will never end, but it always does, sooner or later. Things change rapidly. Suddenly, the sun feels too hot, and the salt burns your eyes.

We drifted for two more hours, fishless, before returning to the harbor. Once we got there, my father insisted on having the weakies weighed. I was embarrassed, because I knew they were school fish, not trophies.

The skiff guy slapped them on a bucket scale one at a time. "Five pounds on her," he said, "and four and three-quarters on her."

I asked my father, kidding around, if he could tell which fish was his.

"The big one," he said, carrying her off to the car.

At my place we took photos. The women were polite and made some admiring sounds. There was a discussion about how to cook the fish. My brother wanted to cut them into steaks and barbecue them; my father thought they'd be better if they were filleted and baked. I consulted Alan Davidson's *North Atlantic Seafood,* an extraordinary compendium of marine and gastronomic information. Davidson says, "A good fish, when fresh-caught; a bit flabby later on. The flesh is lean and flaky. Weaks may be grilled whole or pan-fried or used in fish chowders."

I read aloud Davidson's recipe for pan-frying.

"We should cut them into steaks," my brother said, "and barbecue them."

Family has its own peculiar and rewarding flow.

. . .

Before I left my rented house, I stopped in to say good-bye to O'Neill. I told him I never did manage to catch a weakfish in the surf. O'Neill said I shouldn't worry—the experience would stand me in good stead on future trips.

"You going back to California now?" he asked.

"Not yet," I said. "First, I'm going up to Saratoga for some racing. After that, I might go to Europe."

"You won't catch nothing overseas, kiddo. You think you'll ever come back this way?"

I told him I probably would. I'd become attached to Long Island again; I'd made a kind of peace.

"Then I better show you these lures I just got in," O'Neill said, pulling open a drawer.

Horse-trading
at Saratoga Springs

Around racetracks, it's common knowledge that quality thoroughbreds have become a fashionable investment among people with money to burn, but I didn't understand how or why this had happened until I went to the Fasig-Tipton Company's sixty-first annual yearling sales, held during the New York Racing Association's summer meeting at Saratoga Springs. Fasig-Tipton is the Sotheby Parke Bernet of yearlings—it has annual gross receipts of about $200 million, on which the firm earns a five per-cent commission—but even John M. S. Finney, its astute president, did not anticipate the riot of conspicuous consumption that occurred while I was there. In the course of four glittering evening sessions, I watched Finney and his tuxedo-clad auctioneers sell off two hundred and thirty-eight head of prime racing stock for a total return of $38,220,000. The average price per yearling was $160,000—an astonishing fifty-thousand-dollar increase over the previous year's average.

Saratoga has a history of wretched excess. Even before there was a racetrack, gamblers and swells came to town to play faro and roulette, attend grand society balls, and take the healing waters at a variety of spas that offered many strange and wonderful treatments. Indians had been touting the curative properties of the mineral springs around Saratoga for centuries, but the locals didn't start dipping in their toes until the eighteenth century. The first was William Johnson, an Irish baronet, who crossed the ocean in 1738 to manage his uncle's estates in New York. Johnson had a sterling career as a soldier and an administrator, and, eight years after his arrival, he was appointed Commissary of New York for Indian Affairs. The Iroquois were supposedly quite fond of Johnson, and he returned their fondness in traditional colonial style by acquiring several Iroquois mistresses and fathering over a hundred illegitimate children by them.

In middle age, Johnson contracted gout. He also had some referred pain from an old battle wound—a bullet was still lodged in one of his legs. Molly Brant, who was a sister to Joseph Brant, the great Mohawk chief, arranged for him to visit High Rock Spring and be treated for his ailments. Johnson took a boat down the Mohawk River to Schenectady. He could not walk very well, so native bearers had to carry him on a litter to High Rock. Johnson spent four days there, in a bark hut, undergoing a strict regimen that included copious interior and exterior applications of spring water. His health improved so much that the Indians only had to carry him part of the way home. "I have just returned from a visit to a most amazing spring, which almost effected my cure," he wrote to a friend. Later visitors to High Rock shared Johnson's enthusiasm. By 1821, the springs in Saratoga were famous, and a guidebook from that year listed the most popular spas and the diseases they might be expected to meliorate:

Jaundice and bilious affections generally, Dyspepsia, Habitual Costiveness, Hypochondriacal Complaints, Depraved appetite, Calculous and nephritic complaints, Phagendic or ill conditioned ulcers, Cutaneous eruptions, Chronick Rheumatism, Some species or states of gout, Some species of dropsy, Scrofula, paralysis, Scorbutic affections and old scorbutic ulcers, Amenorrhea, Dysmenorrhea and Chlorosis.

Thoroughbred racing was added to the enticements of Saratoga in August 1863. The person responsible was John Morrissey, a fine heavyweight boxer, also Irish, who'd parlayed his connection to the Dead Rabbits gang on the Bowery into a life in New York politics. Morrissey had been a pimp and a hired thug as well as a fighter. He financed his political campaigns with the proceeds from his investments in faro parlors—he had sixteen of them scattered around Manhattan. When Morrissey decided to come to Saratoga on holiday, he brought some card dealers and faro tables with him and set up a parlor on Matilda Street, near all the best hotels. His operation was an instant hit, but he reckoned that his wealthy customers might be induced to spend even more lavishly if they had a racetrack around to amuse them.

The track Morrissey used for his first meeting was called Horse Haven. It was located on rough land in the pine woods. The meeting lasted for four days only, with just two races on each day's card. Horses were in somewhat short supply, since most healthy animals had been conscripted into the Union and Confederate forces to help fight the Civil War. Morrissey's venture was a success anyway, largely because he had the good sense to involve men like William

Travers in it. Travers was a highly respected stockbroker and bon vivant who belonged to twenty-seven clubs and had unimpeachable ties to the society crowd. He became the first president of the Saratoga Racing Association. In August 1864, the association transferred its meeting to a new track across the road from Horse Haven. The inaugural Travers Stakes was run that year; a Travers-owned horse, Kentucky, won it. The grandstand at the new track was bigger, the racing strip was wider, and everybody was pleased. Since then, many changes have been made in the plant, but races have been held continuously, and the course is counted as the oldest still in use in the United States.

Saratoga Springs lies about thirty miles north of Albany, in the foothills of the Adirondacks. I drove up there from Long Island on a brilliantly clear afternoon in August. Although the sun was hot, there was a touch of autumn in the air; frosts can come early in the mountains. I got off the Thruway outside the town proper and followed a map that my hosts had drawn for me. It led me past farms and woods, then past a murky slough where two men in overalls were fishing for bullheads—snub-nosed catfish that thrive in even the most polluted streams. I could see Saratoga Lake in the distance. It's a substantial body of water that's now a tangle of moss and water hyacinths. Once, it held a large population of native trout, but resort owners who had hotels and cabins along the shore stocked it with pickerel and black bass, and the trout were soon cannibalized. The bass showed up as a specialty on resort menus, cooked over a fire and basted with an upstate version of *beurre noir*.

The house that my hosts had rented for the duration of

the month-long meeting could have been a remnant of one of those vanished resorts. It had a screened porch and a crabgrassy little yard. After I put my bag in the guest bedroom, I tried to make some small talk about matters unrelated to thoroughbreds, but I learned quickly that this was a breach of etiquette, and I confined all my later remarks to equine affairs. In the morning, I was given a *Daily Racing Form* with my coffee and told to be ready for an eleven o'clock departure for the track. The convoy left right on time. We were in town by noon. The streets were jammed with hundreds of Nature-drunk punters from Manhattan who were thumping their chests to make space in their lungs for the unfamiliar fresh air. They were as tanned and carefree as kids on vacation, and so were the trainers and jockeys I saw in the paddock before the first race. Saratoga was apparently like every other summer camp in the Adirondacks, except that it catered to adult horse fiends. The pressures of urban life had been suspended or forgotten, and nobody seemed to be taking things very seriously.

Saratoga is one of the few rural tracks in the United States where you can see absolutely first-rate racing. The stars of Belmont and Aqueduct are in attendance, along with a few outliers from Kentucky, Florida, and southern California. The atmosphere is a mix of county fair and chautauqua. You can buy apples and peaches from farm-girl concessionaires, and there's a fountain beneath a vintage pergola that dispenses, absolutely free, the fabled waters of the Big Red Spring. The horses are saddled under the pines and elms, then brought to the paddock, and this adds to the casualness of the place. Some of the bettors become so relaxed that they actually take naps between races, stretched out on blankets in the midst of picnic scraps and empty wine bottles. If you're in a hurry to get to the windows, you have to watch that you don't step on anybody's hands or face. All racetracks exist at a considerable remove from reality, but Saratoga is definitely the king.

This spirit of unreality was also reflected in the Fasig-Tipton yearling sales. Admission to the sales was by invitation only, but my hosts had finagled tickets, and, after dinner that first night, they had me put on my sport coat and then took me to the Humphrey S. Finney Sales Pavilion—a crate-like modern building that's located across from the racetrack on a few acres of land that Fasig-Tipton owns. Inside the pavilion, there are eight hundred red auditorium seats arranged in a scallop that faces a horseshoe-shaped auction ring. The ring is bounded by ropes threaded through iron hitching posts; it could have been used for one of Morrissey's prizefights. The best seats, close to the ring, are given to Fasig-Tipton's best and oldest customers. Balcony seats generally go to infrequent bidders and what Fasig-Tipton calls "nontraditional interests"—people who've made a sudden fortune in auto parts or missile nose cones and must divest themselves of extra cash or pay it to the government in taxes. Spectators like us got to stand behind the balcony seats and observe things from a distance.

Promptly at eight-thirty, John Finney stepped onto a wooden platform near the auction ring and seated himself in the kind of bar chair you find in country clubs. He nodded politely to the audience, to his auctioneer, and to six men in black tie. The men were bid spotters. They were stationed at strategic intervals around the room, so that they could

translate the audience's ear tugs and cheek pulls into bids
and then relay them—usually by whooping—to the auctioneer. At the previous night's sales, the bidders had shown
a marked ability to spend money at a record-breaking pace,
and Finney decided to poke some fun at them. He an-
nounced that the local police had informed him that a group
in favor of redistributing American wealth had been granted
a permit to hold a peaceful demonstration outside the pavilion. "I thought we'd been trying to redistribute the wealth
all week long," said Finney, deadpan, his glasses slipping
down his nose.

This provoked a lot of laughter, but the laughter was
transformed into awe when Woody Stephens, a Hall of
Fame trainer bidding on behalf of Hickory Tree Farm, in
Virginia, shelled out a million dollars for the first yearling to
appear in the auction ring—a dark bay colt by the two-time
Prix de l'Arc winner Alleged out of the Sea-Bird mare Gulls
Cry. Stephens's purchase was topped later in the evening
when E. P. Taylor, a prominent Canadian breeder, paid
$1,200,000 for a chestnut filly by The Minstrel (winner of
the 1977 Epsom and Irish derbies) out of Directoire. Even
the most jaded bidders seemed to tremble a bit when the
filly—now valued at about eleven hundred dollars a
pound—was led away, back to her stall on the Fasig-Tipton
compound, where she'd wait for a van to take her to her new
home, Windfields Farm, Taylor's spread on Maryland's
Eastern Shore.

The inflationary spiral we were witnessing at Saratoga
really began in the mid-1970s. Until then, the practice of
speculating in horses had been confined to professionals,
and to old-line racing families, like the Phippses and the

Whitneys. But the glamour of the sport, along with its significant investment advantages, has gradually attracted more and more nontraditional interests—the phrase suggests the Great Unwashed—to the bidding arena. For them, as well as for the Phippses and the Whitneys, racehorses represent a tax shelter of no mean proportions. According to the Internal Revenue Service, a yearling may be presumed to have a "useful life" of five years; during that period an owner may annually deduct twenty per cent of the yearling's purchase price, and also any expenses related to racing—food, training costs, veterinary bills, travel, and so on. Real estate barons get a similar break when they buy a string of condominiums, but condos have little prestige value compared with the offspring of Hoist the Flag.

There are other possible benefits from investing in racehorses. A yearling, as a colt or filly, may perform well on the track and earn a few hundred thousand dollars in purses. A handful of extremely talented colts will develop into candidates for the jackpot known as syndication, which can bring lucky owners millions in profit. Syndication is the process by which shares in a colt about to be bred (he's called a stallion now) are offered to selected investors—often breeders and other individuals who know the value of quality horseflesh. The shares are ordinarily sold in units of forty, and the holder of one share is entitled to use the stallion's services for one mare or to sell them to somebody else during the breeding season, which occurs in spring and early summer. Stud fees can be considerable if the stallion is fertile and his offspring are successful—sometimes upward of a hundred thousand per mating—and continue to pour in until the stallion gives up the ghost: ten or fifteen years, maybe.

Some enthusiastic studs, like Nashua, who was twenty-nine and still ready to go, last even longer. The market value of brood mares is not so high—a mare delivers only one foal every season, while a stallion can cover as many as sixty mares—but a pretty penny can be turned on a filly who has raced decently and has desirable bloodlines.

All this means gravy for Fasig-Tipton. In 1981, the firm conducted forty-six horse auctions, in seven states and Canada. The Saratoga sales have always been the most prestigious and rigidly controlled. Breeders who want to have their yearlings included must nominate them by the first of March. Fasig-Tipton's experts then grade the pedigrees on a scale of one to ten. Yearlings who pass the test are subjected to an exhaustive physical examination and graded again on the same scale. They must achieve a minimum combined rating of eight to qualify for Saratoga. Once a yearling has been accepted, its breeder signs a contract with Fasig-Tipton: the breeder agrees to pay a small penalty if the yearling is withdrawn from sale, except for a veterinary reason, and Fasig-Tipton agrees, among other things, not to sell the yearling for less than ten thousand dollars. In late July, the yearlings are vanned to Saratoga—they come primarily from Kentucky, Virginia, Maryland, Florida, and New York—and stabled in Fasig-Tipton's barns.

One afternoon, I toured the barns. The famous outfits, like Spendthrift and Newstead Farms, had taken over entire shed rows, and decorated them with color-coordinated feed tubs, potted flowers, and brightly painted signs advertising the choicest items in their lines. Consignors who were handling the stock of four or five small breeders did their best to

compete, but there was something of the visiting poor relation about them. It was odd how the usual odors of the
backstretch—manure, sweat, liniment—had somehow gotten expunged from the barns. Instead, I smelled soap and
perfume. Every now and then, I saw a groom bring out a
yearling for the inspection of potential customers, including
narrow-eyed bloodstock agents. Each yearling wore an
identifying number on its halter. The grooms were cleaner
than any grooms I've ever seen. Some of them were required to wear Izod Lacoste shirts and khaki trousers—a
preppy uniform that I read as an unintentional act of par-
ody. But the yearling inspections were still conducted in
dead earnest, since Fasig-Tipton sells every horse "as is";
title passes to the buyer at the fall of the auctioneer's hammer.

So the Fasig-Tipton sales became an integral part of my
stay at Saratoga. Every evening, I put on my sport coat,
joined the other idle spectators behind the balcony seats,
and watched the auction. There was always a steady stream
of gossip going on. In it, I could hear echoes of that star-
struck "Middle Western" youth Nick Carraway, who once
wrote the names of guests who'd come to Gatsby's fancy
parties in the margins of his railroad timetable. I had no
timetable, only a *Racing Form,* but on it I noted that
Thomas Mellon Evans, Pleasant Colony's owner, came to
the sales in a powder-blue blazer and beige slacks. Mrs.
Cloyce Tippett, of Llangollen Farm, came in a raspberry
caftan studded with gold sequins. Ogden Mills (Dinny)
Phipps came, and so did Mrs. C. V. Whitney, who threw a

splashy ball. Helen Alexander, the King Ranch heiress, was there, and so was Dolly Green, whose father founded Beverly Hills. The Indian shipping magnate Ravi Tikkoo came with his associate, Peter Howe. And then there was Sheikh Mohammed bin Rashid al-Maktoum, son of the ruler of Dubai, who came with an entourage of family and servants and bought many fine animals for his racing-and-breeding operation, Aston Upthorpe Stud, in Berkshire, England.

The pattern of the auction didn't change much from evening to evening. It always began with John Finney taking his seat in the bar chair and delivering some prefatory remarks. Then a groom led the first yearling to be sold from the outside paddock to the pavilion door and turned it over to a Fasig-Tipton handler—sallow men in starched white jackets and loose-fitting trousers that made them look like stewards on an ocean liner bound for the Balkans. The handler took the yearling through the door and into the ring. This was always a bad moment for the horse, to move from semi-darkness into brilliant artificial light. Some yearlings whinnied; others reared or bucked. A few defecated and then an old black man dressed like the handlers came out with a shovel to clean up the mess.

When the yearling started to quiet, Finney would read its pedigree in orotund, preacherly tones before letting the auctioneer cut loose. The bid spotters' heads bobbed up and down; they whooped and cajoled. The auctioneer carried on a sweet, rhythmical, singsong patter, registering the bids and asking for more. If things slowed down, Finney jumped in to remind his audience that they were about to miss an extraordinary opportunity to purchase a yearling of such high caliber that it could not possibly disappoint. And then the auctioneer would pick up his cadence again, wheedling and cajoling, drawing out the affair until an acceptable conclusion was reached. *Bang!* went the hammer on a disk of wood, and yearling No. 201, a chestnut colt by Nijinsky II out of Fast Line, was sold to Dolly Green for four hundred thousand dollars. Minutes later, a new yearling was in the ring, glancing around in bafflement.

It was in this smooth and effortless fashion that the two hundred and thirty-eight yearlings were married to investors. The only crack in the continuity occurred on the final evening of the sales, when the demonstration that Finney had alluded to actually took place. A small group of protesters marched from nearby Congress Park to the front doors of the pavilion. They called themselves RAM—Redistribute America Movement. They were mostly young, except for a black woman in a wheelchair and a middle-aged war veteran on crutches, and they handed out mimeographed circulars. Their leaders claimed that the Fasig-Tipton auction would generate more than $1,800,000 in tax write-offs for the rich people at Saratoga, while federal budget cuts were taking away $400,000 from the poor people in the area. It was difficult to tell how the figures had been arrived at, but the question underlying them was clear: How can so much money be thrown away on horses when so many human beings are struggling to stay alive? The question went unanswered, as it always does, and the protesters were ignored or rebuked. Nobody entering the pavilion seemed the slightest bit embarrassed by their presence. In the morning, on my way to the track, I found their circulars all over the Fasig-Tipton compound—in trash cans, on tables and chairs, fallen everywhere indiscriminately, like leaves.

TWO

ENGLAND
AND ITALY

I find the Englishman to be him
of all men who stands firmest
in his shoes. They have
in themselves what they value
in their horses—mettle and bottom . . .
—Ralph Waldo Emerson, *English Traits*

Florence pleased us for a while.
—Mark Twain, *Innocents Abroad*

❦ ❦

At The Fountain

An English person chooses a local pub in a deeply complex and emotional way, forming a bond that will last for life, so when my wife and I arrived in England and rented a flat on Myddelton Square, in the North London borough of Islington, I approached the problem of choosing my own local with an attitude that combined high seriousness and moral purpose. The first pub I tried was Crown and Woolpack, just around the corner from the square. It was a decent enough place, although dingy around the edges and somewhat humorless in character. The cheese rolls were sometimes stale. The barman I dealt with was a tough, unsmiling mug from Manchester whose presence was only slightly mitigated by that of a sunny young woman who came in to help with lunch and looked exceptional in jeans. In retrospect, I think the only reason I stayed with Crown and Woolpack for so long was that it occupies a minor niche in the history of revolutionary politics. Vladimir Lenin once lived in a room above it, back when the pub was part of an inn. A plaque on the pub wall says that a London police constable was stationed in the room next to Lenin's and instructed to listen in on any suspect, proto-Communist conversations that might occur.

The constable heard plenty, but he caused a furor at head-quarters when he was asked to report, because, as he explained to his stunned superiors, he understood no Russian.

After a while, I got tired of Crown and Woolpack and shifted my allegiance to The Old Red Lion, down the block. The Old Red Lion was very clean. It housed a fledgling the-ater company in an upstairs auditorium, but the tavern area downstairs was too large and never became crowded enough to produce the special feeling of intimacy and bonhomie that I consider the hallmark of a good bar. The best thing about The Old Red Lion (at least from a spectator's stand-point) was that somebody there owned a dog who was mas-terful at chasing after bags of potato chips—or crisps, as the British call them. The barman or barmaid would grab a bag from a handy rack behind the bar and toss it onto the floor, and the dog would tear after it, pin it down with his paws, rip open the cellophane with his teeth, and devour the contents. He never left a chip. This was an evolved dog who had learned to accommodate—no, *appreciate*—the junk food effluvia of the century. If his master had been able to teach him to drink a pint of beer while he was eating, I might have signed on forever at The Old Red Lion, but the chip-chasing stunt, as spectacular as it was, did not, in the end, bind me to the joint.

From The Old Red Lion, I moved on to Blue Coat Boy, but it was located right next to the Angel tube stop, and it had the sort of clientele you might find in a Blarney Stone off Forty-second Street shortly after midnight when the rain is falling and only people with ink in their veins are willing to venture outside. During my brief tenure at Blue Coat Boy, I was in constant fear that a random fist was about to separate my teeth from my gums, so I moved again, this time to The Agricultural, which was close to Chapel Market—a wonderful street market where I bought spuds, cabbages, and "knobby" brussels sprouts from cockney vendors whose poor pink fingers protruded from wool gloves that had been snipped off at the knuckles. At Chapel Market, the King Edward potatoes were always "new," and the onions were always "sound." On weekends, when the market was thronged with people buying shoes, bras, reggae records, prawns, cockles, whelks, eel pies, streaky bacon, chips, fried skate, fried plaice, fried sole, pet supplies, greeting cards, brilliant oranges from Haifa, and a thousand other items both useful and frivolous, there was a man who strolled around with a monkey on his shoulder, introducing himself to children. Some of this raucous spirit filtered into The Agricultural, but I finally decided it was too far from home, and, reluctantly, I gave it up.

Next, I hit The Harlequin, set back in an alley just paces from the stage door of Sadler's Wells Theatre, a venue for opera and ballet. The first night I went in, I had a pleasant conversation with the barman, who told me that a customer of his, a writer, had recently published a biography of Edith Sitwell. This was pretty high-tone stuff after the talk of vegetable prices over at The Agricultural. The Harlequin had a semisophisticated atmosphere. Ballerinas drank there, but so did stagehands, ordinary Joes, and neighborhood sots with monumental noses. It might have been perfect, in fact, except that it also attracted a large number of uptown balletomanes who wandered in on the chance that they might rub elbows with a star. They gathered in corners and gave off a mist of sensitive understanding. Sometimes the mist inside The Harlequin got so thick that it made breathing difficult, and once again, on the point of attachment, I was forced to look elsewhere for satisfaction.

Across the street, I discovered The Shakespeare's Head. It had all the charm of a suburban parlor in Brighton, adorned as it was with knickknacks and quaint photographs, including one of John F. Kennedy. A large television console held a position of honor in the room. It rested on a stool and confronted the patrons in such a way that it seemed to be demanding obeisance. I was always thinking I should throw some coins to it, or otherwise acknowledge its power, so I quit hanging around The Shakespeare's Head—what was a TV *doing* in a pub named for the Bard?—and moved on to The Empress of Russia, where folk music groups performed once a week. There was nothing particularly wrong with The Empress of Russia, but there was nothing particularly right with it, either. It felt middle-class, well-fed, and complacent, and that put me off a little. Besides, in order to reach it, I had to cross a busy intersection near Sadler's Wells, and I became concerned that a speeding truck might run me down as I strolled back to the flat after closing time.

I traveled next to The Percy Arms on Great Percy Street, which was compact and friendly but somehow down on its luck; and then to Merlin's Cave, which was dark and dank and afflicted with kids who kept playing terrible Human League syntho-pop over and over again on the jukebox; and then to Marler's, which was alarmingly like a California singles' bar, featuring brunettes instead of blondes. I began to despair that I would ever find a pub that really appealed to me, and then, quite by accident, as I was knocking about one evening, I noticed The Fountain on the corner of Amwell and Ingelbert Streets and stuck my head inside and sealed my fate.

Islington is the most densely populated borough in London. Some people maintain that it's also the ugliest. Wherever you go, you see industrial textures. The predominant colors are gray, brown, black, and, occasionally, the faded red of weathered bricks. There aren't many trees around, except in squares. Buildings are beat-up, ancient, grimed with soot, and often in such dishabille that it's impossible to tell whether they're being renovated or demolished. In the public mind, Islington has become synonymous with the word "gentrification"——that is, the process by which members of the gentry take over and transform a district previously occupied by members of the lower classes. Other North London boroughs, like Camden Town and Kentish Town, have already been largely colonized by doctors, dentists, barristers, and other professionals who could not afford the inflated real estate prices in more fashionable London boroughs, like Belgravia, Mayfair, Chelsea, or Kensington.

In an effort to prevent the same thing from happening in Islington, the Islington Council, an elected body known to be cantankerous and left-leaning (if not downright anarchic), has acquired property throughout the borough with an eye to eventually fixing it up and then renting flats to low-income individuals and families, thereby keeping the neighborhood heterogeneous. The plan is an honorable one, but the council has constantly found itself short in the pocket, unable to produce the necessary fix-up funds, so squatters have moved into many of the vacant properties. They use a paperback squatters' handbook to learn how to jerry-rig the toilets and electricity, and they pay no rent. This outrages there'll-always-be-an-England types, who think that it's unfair to exploit the system instead of letting the system exploit you.

Among the most gentrified areas in Islington are Canonbury, where the young Evelyn Waugh kept himself pickled, and the streets near Camden Passage, where old buildings have been converted into an arcade of boutiques, antique shops, and dear little restaurants. Myddelton Square ranks considerably below these spots in terms of trendiness. Professionals do live on the square, but so do squatters, laborers, retired people, junkies, and owners of marginal businesses. It is a rare and special place—quiet, unassuming, dignified, and somehow locked into the rhythms of the previous century. The four-story row houses that enclose the square were built between 1821 and 1827. They are brown brick, with white-coved windows and fanlighted doors. The doors are painted blue, yellow, dark green, or red, and they seem to glow with the suggestion that lives of uncommon richness and diversity are being lived behind an anonymous facade.

In the building where my wife and I settled, there were ten flats. Ours was on the top floor. It was small, with two bedrooms and a tiny kitchen into which two average-size adults had trouble squeezing. It had no central heating, only little electric blow heaters, so we were always cold. Its greatest virtue was that it looked out on the square and St. Mark's Church. St. Mark's is a curiosity. It was built by an engineer, not an architect, and there is something sturdy and indomitable about it. It gave us a feeling of abiding safety. From our living room windows, we often watched children playing on swings and slides in the churchyard, while idlers sat nearby on pigeon-dappled benches. A gardener was always working on the grounds. He laid new sod where frost had damaged the grass, and tended to his rosebushes. The bushes, stripped of their greenery, were brittle and wan, but even in November a few stubborn red and yellow roses were still clinging to the branches.

The square was named for Sir Hugh Myddelton, who was born in Wales about 1560. His parents sent him to London to become a goldsmith, and he was very successful at his trade. Myddelton also dabbled in seagoing ventures, encouraged by his friendship with Sir Walter Raleigh and other captains. Early in the seventeenth century, when London's water supply from the Thames began to run low, Myddelton volunteered to implement a government plan to tap some springs at Chadwell and Amwell, in Hertfordshire, and bring the overflow to the city by means of a conduit. The project was completed on Michaelmas Day in 1613. The rechanneled springs were known as the New River, and a holding company was formed to manage it. Myddelton, who died poor in spite of his labors, went back to his goldsmith's shop. It was said that he and Raleigh used to sit on the shop steps and smoke the newly introduced weed tobacco, much to the amusement of passersby.

Because the square is so self-contained, it approximates

in its turnings the pace of old village life. We could buy almost anything we needed within a half-mile radius. For milk
and butter, we went to Mr. Lloyd, a Welshman like Myddelton. Mr. Lloyd is sixty-seven and nearly as broad as he is
tall. He was always dressed in a white shirt, topped by a gray
V-neck sweater, topped by a maroon V-neck sweater. A
striped blue apron was always tied around his ample waist.
He wore spectacles on the tip of his nose, and when he scur-
ried around the neighborhood in his shopkeeper's costume,
he looked like a refugee from a road company of *Alice in
Wonderland*. Mr. Lloyd used to own a dairy—Islington was
once a dairy center. He got up at three in the morning to fill
bottles with milk trucked in from the countryside. His employees earned three quarts of milk per day in addition to
their wages. Empty Lloyd's Dairy bottles gather dust in Mr.
Lloyd's windows. The best milk available at the shop is Jer-
sey milk, distinguished by its gold cap and floating plug of
cream. "Builds bonny babies," Mr. Lloyd liked to say as he
toted up our bill on the back of a brown paper sack.

Across from Mr. Lloyd's, there was a greengrocer's
where we bought fruit and vegetables whenever our weekly
haul from Chapel Market ran low. On the next block was
George Carter's butcher shop. At Carter's, turkeys hung by
their feathered necks above gammon steaks, English lamb
chops, and trays of deliquescent veal. Our butcher, Ted, was
bald and skinny, with dark circles under his eyes. He was
fond of hard rock music, and it was not unusual to see him
lay down a few jukey steps to a radio tune while he was
hacking the neck off a chicken. His wife, Maureen, from
whom he was separated, was a clerk at A. R. Dennis & Co.,

Ltd., Turf Accountants——the betting shop next door. The books on their romance were not officially closed. Sometimes I could tell how it was going by how Maureen acted when I stopped in to make a bet. If things were good with Ted, she laughed and joked; if things were bad, she chewed on her lip and fought back the tears.

The only other neighborhood romance we observed was at the tobacconist's where we bought the daily papers. A young Indian couple, recently married, managed the shop. Like us, they had no central heating. He seemed not to care very much, but she was devastated by the freezing temperatures——the coldest winter in thirty-one years!——and half blamed her husband, in the same way that my wife, who took to dressing like Mr. Lloyd, in layer after layer of clothing, half blamed me. Once, when I told the woman that I was from California, in the United States, she asked in a plaintive voice, "But oh! Then why ever did you come *here?*" The notion that anybody would give up sunshine for snow, slush, and urban blight was as unfathomable to her as it was to the bakery lady who sold us bread or to the cashier who sold us tickets to the Merlin Baths. We swam in the icy pool at Merlin, but we never went upstairs to the private cubicles where, for about eighty cents, we could have taken hot baths in gigantic porcelain tubs. If we had died on the square, the job of embalming us would probably have gone to Thomas Treacy, whose funeral parlor was close to Sadler's Wells. The black-bordered shop, with Treacy's name in gilt lettering, was always a sobering sight when I passed it late at night. Through gauze curtains in the window, I could see two plain wood coffins gaping like mouths, and I always quickened my step, striding off in search of sanctuary, some place warm and giving, like my local pub.

The Fountain is a drab brick building with absolutely no redeeming architectural virtues. It could be a factory or yet another in the endless series of row houses that constitutes North London. The only flashy thing about it is its sign, elongated and maroon. The sign bears the name of the pub and also a large painting of a gold urn (*not*, for some reason, a fountain) from which three symmetrical streams of gold beer rise, then fall in utter harmony. Inside, The Fountain is divided into two separate bars—the usual practice in pubs of any size. The public bar, where prices are cheaper by pennies, caters to the workingman. Its fixtures are simple, listing toward battered. It is decorated with old promotional posters for beer and cheese, a mirror that reproduces a vintage beer label, and some typed notes from a concerned patron addressing the question of how to form a darts team. The team did not form during the five months I was a regular.

The tables in the public bar wobble. The banquettes have hard seats. The crowd drinks mostly draft beer—lager, ale, and stout—while over on the other side of the wall, in the saloon bar, or lounge, liquor takes precedence. Originally, saloon bars were created to offer upgraded services and furnishings to higher-class gents who wished to bring in their lady friends without being afraid that some navvy might spill Guinness into their shoes. The Fountain's is a plush room done in reds and golds, with flocked Victorian wallpaper, etched glass, and thickly cushioned chairs. Customers here tend to be older, stauncher, and more conservative than those in the public bar. Traffic between bars is minimal, since the English are among the most habit-prone people on earth. A visit to the saloon bar by a public-side regular is considered to be roughly equivalent to one of Lawrence's forays into Arabia.

The publican, Peter Keith Page, lives with his family in a flat on the second floor. Page is a fiftyish man, slender and well-tailored, whose manner might be described as studiously charming. His mustache and hair are tinged with auburn, and this, along with a sharp nose and chin, makes him look a bit like a fox. He enjoys jokes, subtle conversations, double entendres. When he takes one of his turns behind the bar, he works at a measured pace, often pausing to ask after his patrons' health and well-being. Mrs. Page is a short, dark-haired woman with careworn features. She has a sweet smile that combines weariness with wisdom. The quality of being a "mum" seems ingrained in her, an inescapable part of her destiny. The Pages have several children—not counting regulars in need of mothering. Most of them are grown, but a teenaged daughter and a little boy about eleven still live at home. Sometimes the daughter came downstairs to meet her dates in the pub. The boy often popped in just before bed to grab a snack of potato chips or peanuts. He stood around in his pajamas, talking to the barmen or the barmaid, and there were favored customers to whom he went for gossip about soccer games. This was one of the nicest things about The Fountain—its air of domesticity, the way the lovely insistence of family life kept intruding upon the solitary world of the drinker.

In the old days, most publicans owned their pubs, but that is no longer the case. The Fountain belongs to the Ind Coope brewery, a subsidiary of Allied Breweries, Ltd., and Page runs it for H. H. Finch, a management company, in exchange for a salary, his flat, and a share of the profits. Allied is numbered among the so-called Big Six breweries. The others are Bass Charrington, Courage, Scottish & Newcastle, Watney-Mann, and Whitbread Co. Over the past quarter century, these corporations have acquired the many small firms who used to compete for a share of the market, and they now dominate the beer business, just as Anheuser-Busch, Miller Brewing, G. Heileman, and so on dominate it in the United States. The British giants have gone their American counterparts one better by gaining control of their primary retail outlets—the country's pubs. The Big Six now own most of the seventy thousand-plus pubs in Great Britain. In The Fountain, all the beers on draft—with the exception of Guinness, which transcends corporate boundaries and is carried everywhere as the stout of choice—are Ind Coope brands. In a Courage pub, the beers will all be Courage brands.

The advantages of this scheme are obvious and enormous. British drinkers complain vehemently about it, but they are, on the whole, as lazy as the rest of us, and few of them will desert their handy local and walk an extra block or two to a pub where a preferred brand might be on tap. (In North London, Bass pubs are thought to have the best beer; Watney pubs are thought to have the worst.) Pubs that are still independent are known as "free houses," and they offer a very good selection of premium beers that are unavailable

in affiliated pubs. The beers come from little breweries outside the corporate world, and they are strong and well-made
and have not been toned down to meet the bland require-
ments of an imaginary customer's palate.

The question of beer quality, or lack of it, is often discussed in pubs, even as the subject of the inquiry is being
swallowed. In all my hours at The Fountain, I never heard
anybody say that British beer is better now than it was in the
past. Generally speaking, most beer drinkers seem to feel
that since corporations own the pubs and have, as it were, a
captive audience, their devotion to quality could be said to
be non-existent. The most common evidence cited in support of this argument is the great keg beer scandal of the
1960s, which occurred shortly after the corporate takeover
began in earnest. In pubs, the preferred draft is usually bitter ale, a copper-colored, unpasteurized, heavily hopped
brew that varies in alcoholic content from three to five-and-
a-half per cent. It varies in taste, too. Some bitters are tart
on the tongue, with a sour underbite, while others are quite
sweet. Bitter comes to the pub in casks and undergoes a sec-
ondary fermentation in the pub cellar, supervised by an experienced cellarman who monitors temperature, the action
of the yeast, and other important factors. It is such a deli-
cately balanced brew that it must be tapped at exactly the
right moment or its flavor will be ruined. The beer, never
carbonated, rises to the bar via a manual pump system. The
barman or barmaid pulls a handle, and out it flows, a half
pint per stroke.

It takes time, care, energy, and a great deal of craft to
make traditional cask-conditioned bitter ales, so, not sur-

prisingly, the corporations decided to phase them out and replace them with more cost-efficient products—pristine keg bitters that would be filtered and pasteurized (longer shelf life), carbonated (less fragile and easier to tap), and brewed to be served cold (masks the flavor). Keg bitters would also have the advantage of requiring minimal care. An inept cellarman could knock over a keg, roll it around, thump it like a conga drum, and still not destroy the beer. Moreover, keg bitters, being uniform and widely distributed, would lend themselves to national rather than regional advertising.

This sounds like the perfect corporate ploy, but the British public—habit-prone, raised on notions of quality—was not so easily led astray. Almost as soon as keg bitters were introduced, a massive revolt began against them. What *was* this thin, fizzy, foul-smelling, vile-tasting dishwater spitting from the taps? In joking protest, some drinkers banded together and mounted what became known as the Campaign for Real Ale, or CAMRA. Their primary demand was that breweries reinstate old-fashioned bitter and forget about this other swill. When CAMRA received coverage in the media, its founders learned that there were millions of disgruntled customers who wanted to join them in applying pressure to the Big Six. The Campaign started publishing an annual guide to good beers, which included a directory of the pubs that stocked them. Eventually, the breweries were forced to give in, and they scrapped their plans for dominion. Every decent pub in London now offers at least one brand of cask-conditioned bitter—*real ale,* that is. Keg bitters are still on draft, but they are ignored by all except the dull, the unrepentant, and the perverse.

. . .

The real ale I most often drank at The Fountain was Burton, a rich, soothing beer named in honor of the town of Burton-on-Trent, which has been a brewing center for hundreds of years. Ind Coope moved there in 1853 after acquiring the famous Allsopp Company. The Allsopps had been making ale since the Crusades. The water in Burton-on-Trent is special, with a high gypsum content that's ideal for pale, sparkling brews. Ale produced in the Burton style is sometimes called India Pale Ale—a relic of colonial days.

I still remember the first glass of Burton I ever had, on that first night I peeked into the public bar. The homey radiance of the place drew me in. I hung my coat on a knob of polished brass and claimed a vacant stool. Right away, a bushy-haired man who'd been doing some kind of puzzle in the *Evening Standard* jumped up from a chair behind the bar and asked me what I wanted to drink. This was John, the cellarman. I say "cellarman" rather than "barman" because John always made that distinction when he talked about his job. He wanted people to know that he had responsibilities beyond the mere drawing of beer. A meticulous person of twenty-eight, John had a vaguely military bearing that manifested itself in a desire for order. Often, he wore a short-sleeved shirt with epaulets, and when he marched from tap to tap, or descended into the cellar to check on the pressure of his kegs, the huge bunch of keys that dangled from his belt loop rattled like the notes of a martial air. An empty glass never lingered on a table when John was around. He'd grab it up and wash it before it had the slightest chance to offend. It was John's dream that Page would someday recommend him to Ind Coope as a potential publican, so he was dedicated and loyal and worked hard to see that The Fountain was congenial and well-run. Like Page, he was quick with a quip—annoyingly so, if you happened to be nursing a sore head and preferred a dose of silence with your beer. Also, he bore an uncanny physical resemblance to his boss. For a while after I started coming in, I assumed he was one of Page's sons. "Not *likely*, mate," he snorted when I asked him about it, but I think that secretly he was pleased to have an attachment—however tenuous—to family.

I told John that I'd like a pint of bitter. "Try the Burton," he said. "It's going very nicely." I watched as he drew my pint—eighteen-plus ounces of beer. (The pint measure derives from an old measure for corn.) He filled the glass right to the top, as required by law. The glass was tall and had no handle. It looked a bit like a Coke glass, although it was twice as big and not quite as nipped in at the middle. Pints are also served in squat, dimpled mugs *with* handles, but such mugs are thought to be on the sissy side of life, and some men won't accept them. Ordering a half pint also smacks of effeminacy, since custom dictates that half pints are for women.

I sipped the Burton. It didn't remind me of any of the other bitters I'd sampled on my rounds. It was softer and milder, with a complex flavor that kept developing nuances on the tongue. The prevailing myth about British beers is that they are served warm, but this isn't true. Pub cellars are cool, particularly in winter. The Burton was not as icy as an average American draft, but it wasn't tepid, either. "That's sweeter than Taylor-Walker," John said, referring to the other real ale that Ind Coope makes. When I tried Taylor-

Walker a few days later, I thought it was thinner-tasting than Burton, with more bite.

Four other drafts are available in the public bar——Double Diamond, Long Life, Guinness, and Skol. Skol is billed as a lager, but that's deceptive. It has none of the clean crispness of German lagers, nor any of the soda-poppy effervescence of American brews. Instead, it's thick and syrupy, conspicuously lacking an edge. For me, it held all the attraction of thirty-weight motor oil. Some people like to spike it with a jigger or two of Rose's Lime Juice. The concoction is known as lager-and-lime, and it is even more sludge-like than unadulterated Skol. Draft Guinness moves slowly at The Fountain, but those who enjoy stout support it vociferously. Stout is stronger than bitter or lager——higher in alcohol, almost black in the glass, and topped with a scurf of foam that tastes healthy when you lift it to your lips. (In Nigeria, where Guinness is revered as a potent sexual elixir, the company slogan used to be *Guinness Gives You Power.*) Bottled Guinness is an entirely different brew, and it attracts a different constituency. It is even thicker and blacker, yielding up a medicinal bouquet. People who swear by it avoid the draft variety on the grounds that it is an inauthentic product. Both Double Diamond and Long Life are examples of the notorious keg bitters that were supposed to sweep the nation. They are not as bad as the British pretend, but they do not compare in any sense to Burton or Taylor-Walker.

When I finished my pint, John drew me another. He wasn't very busy that night. There were only about six customers in the public bar. I asked him if The Fountain was usually so quiet, and he said no——the lack of traffic could be directly attributed to the distance that several regulars were from their next paychecks. Money was tight in Britain, especially among working people, and the Thatcher government seemed determined to tax most stringently their simple pleasures. In the past, anybody with a job could afford a pint or two at the local, but that had changed radically in the last decade. Beer wasn't cheap anymore. Burton went for sixty-four pence a pint, or about a dollar fifteen, and Guinness was ten pence higher. Liquor prices were altogether outrageous. The government insisted that spirits be sold in a standard measure of one-sixth of a gill——about half an ounce. The price of an ordinary whiskey, gin, or vodka was about the same as that for a pint of bitter. John told me that most drinkers of liquor just ordered a double shot instead of mucking around with the singles.

There was a TV in the public bar, mounted near the ceiling, and I asked John what customers liked to watch. Soccer games and horse races, he said. John himself enjoyed a show called "Doctor Who," a science fiction program about outer space types and their intergalactic intrigues. Occasionally, when he had a few minutes to spare, he switched on the set to catch a little of the BBC news. John had a real respect for time——for making the most of it instead of letting it slip away. He often used his free moments behind the bar to do some reading——tales of adventure, detection, espionage, and, of course, sci-fi. One night when I came in, I was shocked to see him reading a paperback copy of John Fowles's *The Magus*. "Pretty heavy business, this is," he said, shaking his head. A week later he was still plugging away, but he complained that Fowles demanded too much concentration, that *The Magus* was dicey in ways that did not necessarily complement the diceyness he had to deal with on the job. Soon enough, the book was laid to rest, consigned to the shelf marked "good intentions." John replaced it with a mystery novel, and, before long, the furrows went out of his brow, and his air of jollity returned.

That John was basically a cheerful person (the English never whine) became clear to me as I drank my second pint. The puzzle he was doing in the *Standard* required him to make as many words as possible from a group of scrambled letters, and he paused every now and then during his cogitation to compliment himself on various acts of deduction. "Take these four letters," he said, showing me the scramble. "N-A-V-E. That's a word, isn't it? Like in a church?" I couldn't resist the challenge, so I copied the puzzle on a bar napkin and went at it. If I hadn't already drunk two pints, I might have been upset at tally time when John proved to have a much higher score than I did. "It's important to have a good vocabulary," he said in a voice that smacked of barely suppressed self-congratulation. He recommended that I have another pint to soften the blow. I protested that a third Burton would push me perilously close to terminal relaxation, but my protest was overruled, and John delivered another draft. "Cheers, Bill," he said. "All the best." By the time I finished it, I was calm and full and ready to tackle any puzzle that might present itself, including the riddle of existence. I said good-bye to John, stepped out into the night, and rolled down Inglebert Street toward the fortress of St. Mark's and the sweet, baffling peace of Myddelton Square.

. . .

So The Fountain became my local pub. What was it that made me so fond of the place? I think in part its very ordinariness. It was local in the deepest and truest sense, a fixed point on the neighborhood compass. Beer was served, but so were news, gossip, attitudes, and opinions. If you were a regular, you stopped in at least twice a day just to keep up with things. These stops were not open-ended for most regulars. They knew in advance how long they'd stay, give or take the odd pint, just as they knew when the fresh scones would come out of the oven at the bakery or when the betting shop would have the results of the late greyhound races from White City. Pubs, with their tightly controlled hours, encourage a rigorous approach to drinking. The midafternoon closure has its roots in the Defence of the Realm Act, passed by the government during the First World War to prevent workers at munitions plants from getting too soused at lunch. Let fumbling fingers aid the Kaiser? Not likely, mate. That DORA is still law seventy years later can be counted as yet another tribute to the British love of the habitual.

The hours at The Fountain could be carved into a granite tablet, so strictly do Page and his staff adhere to them. During the week, the doors open at eleven in the morning and close at three, then open again at five-thirty and close at ten-thirty. On Saturday, the evening opening is pushed back to six o'clock, with a similar half-hour adjustment on the other end. On Sunday, even the grimiest public-side customers dash their cheeks with cologne and put on church suits in anticipation of an alcoholic blitzkrieg that only lasts from noon until two-thirty. Because time is short, drinking is fast, with pints being downed so quickly that Page himself has to pitch in. Luckily, an enforced period of recuperation follows. The Fountain doesn't open again until seven, and its windows go dark for good at half-past ten.

Although I thought of myself as a Fountain regular, I seldom dropped in on weekday afternoons unless I was planning to have lunch——a sandwich from the bakery, or a slab of steak-and-kidney pie that Mrs. Page cooked in her upstairs kitchen. If I had a pint on an empty stomach, as many regulars did, I always wound up staring out the window at the blowing flakes of snow, and I'd remember how cold it was out there——the coldest winter in thirty-one years!——and my hand would begin an involuntary ascent into the air, poking around for John's attention. The refill he brought always ruined me. It undermined the possibility of any reading or writing when I got home and suggested instead that I take a nice cozy nap under a down comforter. Even if I went into the pub with steely resolve, swearing a silent oath to have one pint and no more, I got trapped sometimes by other customers who'd treat me to the second pint before I could refuse. Pub etiquette dictates that the favor be returned, and I'd be stuck. I was afraid I might end up like the Irish bad boys who stayed at The Fountain until the last second and then walked over to A. R. Dennis and killed the sodden hours until the bar opened again by fooling around with Maureen. She seemed to appreciate the break they gave her from the tedium of betting slips and a world-view conditioned by the mesh cage in which she sat.

The restraint I imposed on myself during the day made

me ravenous for beer by early evening. After a quick swim at the Merlin Baths, which created the illusion that I was building up my body faster than I was tearing it down, I bought an *Evening Standard* from the poor frozen Indian woman and proceeded to the pub. If John was on duty, he'd raise an empty glass and ask, "Pint of Burton?" and I'd nod and find the pint resting on a coaster even before I'd hung up my coat. Things did not go as smoothly when Colin was the barman. He was a dreamy lad in his thirties who worked the public side when John was in the saloon bar or taking a rare night off. Colin had been a travel agent once, and he still seemed to be suffering from residual jet lag. He was a friend of the Pages, so he claimed that he wasn't really employed at The Fountain—he was just helping out. He had other contrary ideas as well. "I don't really smoke," he'd say as he slipped a cigarette from somebody's pack on the bar. "It's just to keep my fingers busy."

Colin's lackadaisical style was in marked contrast to John's, and it provided a nice change of pace—although Colin could be forgetful sometimes. One Sunday night, for instance, he forgot to open the pub. I got there at about seven-fifteen and had to join a queue of regulars who were knocking on the locked pub door—rather vehemently, I'll admit, since we were cold and thirsty. Colin finally answered the knocks. He was sleepy-eyed, tousle-haired. He told us he'd fallen asleep on a banquette while watching an old movie on TV. Later in the evening, after Colin had the bar under control, we had a chat about these missed connections. "Amazin', isn't it?" Colin said, smiling and scratching his head. "You get to doing the one thing and you forget all about the others." This was as much a statement of philosophy as a confession of regret, and it endeared Colin to those of us who shared his aptitude for dreaming.

Once I had my pint in hand, whether from John or Colin, I read my *Standard*. It's a tabloid-size paper, heavy on feature stories and columns but lacking the photos of bare-breasted girls that appear on page three of the *Daily Sun*. It functions as an antidepressant, lightening the burdensome weight of the hard and frequently bad news that more serious papers heap on your shoulders every morning. In the evening, you're ready for comic strips, handicapping advice, and the inside scoop on Prince Charles and Lady Di. (She was pregnant then, and the betting shops were offering odds-on in favor of a boy. They were also accepting bets on whether or not Christmas would be white.) After I finished the *Standard*, I ordered another round and sometimes got involved in a game of darts, doing my best to imitate the style of the pro champ of Great Britain, Jocky Wilson. Jocky was a very rotund Scot who admitted to reporters that his recent successes were due to a newfound ability to monitor the amount of beer he drank the night before a tournament. Simply put, Jocky played better when he wasn't hung over. I became fairly adept at darts and learned to throw a set of "arrows" without impaling any bystanders, but what I really liked to do while I nursed my second pint was to talk to people.

It is true that the British are reserved and perhaps seriously repressed, but at The Fountain these characteristics were not so noticeable. I credit the beer. Whiskey tends to sweep the drinker into sudden, unpredictable moods, often of a provocative nature, but good ale or stout loosens the vocables and sets free our hidden desire for intimacy. A glass or two of Burton will make even the shiest person want to lean over and tap the stranger on the next stool. I tapped—or was tapped—many times at the pub, and it seems only fair to provide a brief catalog of some of the people I met, as testimony to Burton's liberating power:

A pen salesman
A poet who published in little magazines
A charwoman
Several construction workers
A Rastafarian who was lost
A hod carrier who had an American friend called "Chicago Bob"
A clerk from a shipping firm
A solicitor
Mr. Lloyd's son, whose name, in my cups, I heard as "Floyd Lloyd"
A girl who sold naughty underwear at a smart boutique in Belgravia
A retired prizefighter who almost punched me because I didn't know anything about Marvin Hagler, the American Middleweight Champ.

Most of these people were just passing through Islington, but there were a few regulars with whom I frequently spoke. One of them was a kid named Colin, who was twenty-six, moon-faced, intelligent, with short, brown, bristly hair that verged toward punk. Once, I heard him refer to himself as Colin Two, to distinguish himself from Colin the barman, and that's how I always thought of him. Colin Two had warm soup for blood. Even in the dead of winter, when the snow lay thick on the ground, he ran around in summery clothes——sometimes just a T-shirt and a sleeveless wool sweater above his trousers. Maybe he could tolerate the cold because he had such a short trip home. He lived with his mother in a council-owned flat above A. R. Dennis. The arrangement was fine, since Colin Two saved money and had somebody to darn his socks and remind him to eat, but he told me that his mother could be tough on him——she was down on his boozing. "She'll only give me enough rope to hang myself," he said. "Then I'm out on my arse."

Recently, Colin Two had been working at a pub on nearby Essex Road as a part-time barman and "dogsbody'" who did odd chores, like mopping up the cellar floor. He'd been made redundant, though——the morbid British way of saying that a position's been terminated. He was considering a new job with a cleaning service. It wouldn't bother him to swab out loos, he said, so long as there was no hassle about it. In a sense, Colin Two was a victim of the Tory economy. Working-class kids like him had no old-boy network to turn to in times of trouble. The only thing Colin really had to look forward to was the onset of spring, when he planned to travel north to Manchester for a visit with his brother. They were going to float down the Thames on a barge, just lying around in the sunshine and knocking back the beer.

Any good local mixes the young with the old. Doug was eighty when I met him. He was waiting for dreamy Colin to bring him his stout, and we struck up a conversation. He invited me to join him at a table he was sharing with his sister, who was eighty-three. She was a shrunken little woman who immediately directed my attention to the black liquid in her glass and introduced me to Mr. Guinness—a pseudo-face in the foam. Mr. Guinness had a hole for a nose, two holes for eyes.

"That's a sign of fresh beer," she said smugly. "Isn't it, Doug?"

"That's a sign of fresh beer," Doug agreed, tugging at the brim of his slouch cap. He gave his sister a bunch of coins, and she wandered off to feed them into the slot machine—it paid out a two-pound jackpot. While she was gone, Doug told me that he had another sister, older still, who liked to go disco-dancing. I didn't doubt it, since Doug was solid evidence of the soundness of his family's stock. He had a steel-trap mind and never missed a trick. He loved jokes more than anything. Whenever he laughed, he'd throw his body back against his chair and expose his pink toothless baby's gums and the old pink tip of his tongue.

"I was in the Meat Game," he told me on another night, gripping my forearm for emphasis. The Meat Game—did I understand? Butcher's business! (Gums, pink tongue.) He'd had his own shop, back in the days when beef was beef. In his spare time, he played the squeeze-box. He even performed at dances at The Fountain, back in the days when . . .

"I always loved music," Doug said.

"Doug always loved music," said his sister.

"I always loved music," Doug said. He took out his wallet and showed me a brown-edged photo of him with an accordion draped around his neck, and then one of him in a soldier's uniform, posed next to his father. The most important one he gave me in secret, passing it under the table. It showed a group of young soldiers, veterans of the Great War, standing on crutches in the middle of a dirt road. They were all missing an arm, or a leg, or both legs. "That's what it was like," Doug whispered, as if the image captured every bit of horror he'd known in his eighty years. But that was the only darkness I ever saw in him, the only wound. He was happy for decent health and a glass or two of stout. "No use in complaining," Doug would say.

Then there was Giustino. He was the most outlandishly generous customer in the pub. Every time I ran into him, he insisted on buying me a beer. If I tried to buy one for him, he'd slap my hand. "No, no, Johnny," he'd say, pursing his lips. I was always Johnny to Giustino. His English was faulty. He hadn't been in the country long. His home village in southern Italy had been destroyed in an earthquake—*"Terremoto,"* Giustino would say, gesturing with his arms to show how the rubble fell, the houses, the people—and afterward he'd started wandering across the continent, working as a chef. He worked now at an excellent restaurant in the financial district. "Good money," he'd say, producing a fat roll of bills to convince me. The cash went for drinks, for luxury items, for *food*—that was Giustino's passion. Every Sunday morning, he shopped at Chapel Market for the big lunch he always cooked for his wife, and he liked to display what he'd bought. "First, *bistecca,*" he'd say, putting a slab of beefsteak on the bar. "Second, some potato. Then, *radicchio* for salad. Lovely." He'd pause to kiss his fingertips. *"Lovely.* Next, some red wine. Some musharoom. Some

broccoli. LOVELY!" Though Giustino had many acquaint-
ances at The Fountain, he confessed to me once, in a despondent mood, that he was lonely. These English, they
were very nice, they treated him decently, but, well—they
were *English,* not Italian. "I need *simpatico,*" Giustino said.

The best friends I made at The Fountain were Simon and
Juliana. I met Simon first, on a drizzly Sunday night, when
he came into the pub and demanded that I give him the magazine I was reading. I glanced over at the next stool and saw
a lean, fidgety young man in jeans and a faded cowboy shirt
who resembled the French actor Jean-Pierre Léaud. I was so
taken aback by Simon's forwardness that I didn't answer
right away. "I just want a bloody look," he said, frustrated
by my hesitation. I handed him the magazine and watched as
he riffled through the pages, searching for something. When
he didn't find it, he rolled up the magazine—rolled it up, I
say—and handed it back. Later, I would learn that it was his
habit to crush, crumple, or otherwise mangle pretty much
every object he touched, the better to file it in a pocket of
his pants.

He asked me if I was aware that I'd purchased a blatantly
centrist rag. A film he'd done some editing on—a documen-
tary about the People's March for Jobs—wasn't even listed
in the cinema section.

I said that I was not aware that I'd purchased a blatantly
centrist rag—that I had in fact found the magazine's listings
to be comprehensive and accurate. I used it whenever I
wanted to go to the movies.

Well, said Simon, running a hand through his long, black

hair, wasn't I the lucky American tourist? He wished that he could go to the cinema now and then, inasmuch as film (not bloody literature) was what he cared about. But he was strapped with this insufferable job at a TV station in South-ampton, slicing up videotape for the evening news. Did I have any idea what sort of town Southampton was? It was a bloody nowhere Navy town, better than an hour's train ride from London. Nobody lived there except drunken sailors and indigent shipbuilders. Was there any chance that I could grasp what it was like to have to spend Monday to Friday in that wasteland? Had I ever boarded in a rooming house full of snoring old sots? The bloody Tories had caused the prob-lem—Maggie Thatcher and her lot. There was hardly any work anywhere in the country. The system was falling apart. And if I thought it was tough on white people, I ought to go out to Brixton and talk to the blacks who lived there—Ja-maicans, Trinidadians, Nigerians, Ghanaians, the poor bloody flotsam of the Empire. Nobody was helping them. It shouldn't come as a surprise to anybody that they'd started putting their feet through the shop windows.

Simon paused here for breath. "We'd better have an-other," he said, calling to John. The Burton came. Simon had light-and-bitter—Burton to which a bottle of light ale had been added. He took a sip, then went into a frenzy. "Oh, no!" he cried. "The laundry." He dashed coatless into the street and returned shortly, shivering. "Forgot the bloody clothes," he said.

Sunday night was laundry night—another in the series of outrageous burdens that Simon had to bear. He was living with a woman, Juliana—they were squatting in an attic room of a row house on the square——and every Sunday, he took his clothes and Juliana's clothes to a laundromat at Amwell Street and then stopped at The Fountain for a pint. About midway through the pint, he'd go back to the laundromat and switch the clothes from washer to dryer. He'd forgotten about the dryer part while we were talking, and it had suddenly occurred to him that some swine had probably removed the clothes from the washer (the laundromat was always overcrowded) and thrown them on the floor——not that he, Simon, would mind, but Juliana preferred clean underthings to ones that had been stomped upon. This penchant for cleanliness did not mean that she was willing to *do* the laundry, of course. Juliana had a pathological aversion to laundromats and wouldn't go near them——something to do with her Irish upbringing, Simon thought, some irrational fear of ending up as a scullery maid. Did I have any idea what it was like to be madly in love with a woman who hated laundromats so much that she expected you to do the bloody wash on your weekend break, when you should have been going to the cinema?

Somewhere in here I ordered two more pints. The beer must have affected me, because pretty soon I was speaking in as loose-tongued a way as Simon, offering a sampler of opinions on love, sex, films, bloody literature, and anything else that floated up to the surface of my mind. Simon drank and listened. I was impressed by his humility, and by the appreciation he showed for my views——at least the Burton I'd drunk made it *seem* like appreciation——and I suggested another round. I think we had another round after this, but I wouldn't swear to it. After a while, the pints lose their discreteness. At ten-thirty, John marched by and took our glasses prisoner, but we agreed that it was imperative to continue our conversation on the following Sunday.

A week went by, and I went back to The Fountain. Simon was already there when I arrived, seated at a banquette with the laundrophobic Juliana. She was about the same age as Simon, in her mid-twenties, wrapped in a tweed greatcoat she'd found in a pub. Her attitude to me was cool, even severe. Who was this American fool? After an hour or so, the beer did its work, and she softened a bit and dropped her guard. She turned out to be witty and tough-minded, locked into a "sorting-out" phase of life. She'd just resigned from an administrative job at the BBC in a dispute over feminist issues, and she was a little confused about what had happened to her and not quite certain what came next. She spent her days in the row house, reading novels both great and trashy, listening to soap operas on the radio, and contemplating—in a half-serious way—her future. She was a brilliant conversationalist, with a hard eye for ironies. It was clear that she was as attached to Simon as he was to her. It made them fun to be around.

I brought my wife on the next weekend, done up in her many layers of protective clothing, and it turned out that we all got along quite well. After that, we began drinking together every Sunday night, convening at a banquette and resting our elbows on a table that became progressively wetter from slicks of spilled beer. The difference in our ages seemed not to matter; in the democratic atmosphere of The Fountain, all but the most essential differences were ignored. When Simon learned that we'd been protest march-ers in our youth, he forgave us for actually paying rent on our flat. We listened to his complaints about the political system, about the world in general, and found that—more often than not—we agreed.

Gradually our friendship pushed its way out of the pub. We invited Simon and Juliana to our place and introduced them to Texas chili. Juliana said that she was amazed to see Simon eat real food—at home, he survived on crisps, like the dog from The Old Red Lion. One night, after the pub closed, they invited us to the squat. We went up to their room by climbing a desperate staircase, past bicycles, boxes of books, and other squatters. There were wires dangling down, exposed bits of insulation. We drank some cans of beer that Simon had stored under the bed, and he sketched some unflattering pictures of us—he'd wanted to be an artist once. The squat was the kind of place that's good to live in when you're young and in love, oblivious to the conditions that will ultimately form the borders of your life. We felt privileged to be there—to be with friends in an improbable country, safe, reasonably warm, in an old stone row house whose windows looked out on a churchyard and those last stubborn roses.

The roses died in mid-December, after a wicked snow-storm. Worst winter in thirty-one years! The Indian woman fell to a constancy of shivering, and Mr. Lloyd put on another sweater. At The Fountain, Christmas decorations went up—strands of gold and silver tinsel across the brass rail of the bar, glittering in the back-bar mirror. The spirit of the season affected the behavior of regulars. There were more toasts more often. The lunch hour stretched into two. John got his hair cut. Ted, the butcher, chased Maureen around with a seltzer bottle, in a conciliatory bout of good cheer.

We went away for the holidays. My brother and his girl flew over for a visit, and we decided to show them the famous English countryside. It was slush, mostly, all the way to Stratford-on-Avon. The Cortina I'd rented kept skidding on icy slicks. Driving the car was like taking a test for brain function. I had to do everything left-handed. Because we share a language with the British, we tend to think we have more in common with them than, say, the Rumanians, but it isn't true. At least the Rumanians know which side of the road to drive on. As we headed southwest, toward the English Channel, the slush was replaced by mud. Near Taunton, in Somerset, there was less mud and more pastureland. Green hills hung with haze. A little lemony sunshine.

Our destination was Chardstock, a tiny village of ancient farms and single-lane roads. Our cottage, plucked from the advertising pages of the *Times,* dated from the fifteenth century. It had a thatched roof, white plaster walls, black shutters, and a little yard. It was trim and pretty. Inside, the plank floors slanted in several different directions, depending on the slope of the land. There were two parlors, both furnished with antiques that were charming but perilous to sit on. The upstairs bedrooms, under the eaves, had rickety beds with quilts and blankets. The woman who owned the place had told us that the heating system—a couple of Dimplex radiators and a vintage space heater—would be inadequate at freezing temperatures, but that she would have a load of wood hauled in. The wood was green. It was wet. We built a fire anyway, using some coal we'd found as kindling, and the cottage filled with smoke. When we opened the windows, frigid air rushed in. Make the best of things, we thought. Be hearty! Thrive in the face of adversity, the way the British do. So we set up the larder, drawing a kind of warmth from its promise. The fresh turkey we'd bought from Ted was already barded with bacon, trussed and ready for the oven. From Harrods we had our Christmas splurge—a haunch of venison that we stuck in an old pot and doused with red wine and bay leaves. The plum pudding went on a sideboard in the fuming parlor, next to bottles of brandy and port.

That done, we walked to the local at the end of the road. We'd noticed it on our way in, the only business in town— The George, it was called. It looked like our cottage, though larger, with the same thatched roof and whitewashed walls. The barroom was small and undivided. It had about three tables, and a bar with a few stools. In an inglenook fireplace, dry logs were blazing. Nobody was in the pub except for a woman who was polishing glasses. "You've come for the carol service," she said, putting her rag down and giving us sheets on which the words to several Christmas carols were printed. We asked for pints and sat on stools to sip them. A man with a ruddy country complexion came in, blowing on his hands. "Come for the carol service, have you?" he asked. He said that it was a custom in the village for families to gather outside The George on the twenty-third of December to await the arrival of Father Christmas, who would ride in on his horse and distribute candy and other trifles to the children. "It's just old farmer so-and-so from over the hill," the man said with a wink. "He's had a few nips at home, and we're hoping he don't fall off the pony."

A crowd began to collect. We joined them, clutching carol sheets and pints. The night air was cold, bloody cold, but the sky was clear and seeded with stars. All around us we saw bundled Chardstockians: red noses, watch caps, tweed coats, steamy breath cycling upward. The kids were bouncing around on their toes, punching one another on the arms. Father Christmas was late. There were more whispered speculations about his sobriety. When he arrived at last, shouting "ho-ho-hos," he looked like a stout Don Quixote, listing to the left in the saddle. His horse was white, and so was his beard. His belly needed no padding. From a sack, he handed out gifts, and the kids squealed and tore paper and compared what they'd got. The carol-singing started. As ever, two or three ringers from the church choir took the lead, and everybody else trailed after them——a junkyard amalgam of broken sopranos and faded tenors. We sang "O Holy Night," "Good King Wenceslaus," and "O Little Town of Bethlehem." Irrepressible emotions. The simplicity of the moment, its utter satisfaction, overwhelmed us. Later, we had whiskey, standing among strangers at the bar, but no longer strange to them, or they to us. Then we walked up the hill to our cottage and ate a cold supper. The sheets on the rickety beds were downright frosty, but we managed to generate some heat——lucky, blessed, thankful for favors.

Farewell to The Fountain. It had to happen sooner or later in the New Year——real life sticking its beak into our affairs. I felt awful to leave London, suffering even before the actual moment of sundering a terrible bout of Burton deprivation——conditioned cells in their infinite craving tossed back on Budweiser or, worse, *Coors.* Would there ever be a proper pub in the States? Not likely, mate. We still needed to learn some of the hard lessons of history, how to be grateful for little things. A good local keeps your nose pressed to essentials. Its rhythms are circadian, recognizable——this small spot in time where burdens are shared and somehow leavened. Sumerian pharmacists prescribed beer for patients, and so did Egyptian doctors, who included it in fifteen per cent of their potions. Anyhow, the neighborhood grows into your bones: roses dead and living, churches, squares. We felt it in ours, a constant pull as we packed our bags, all sad-eyed and unwilling to contemplate the future. The Sunday bus to Luton airport left at one o'clock, so I ducked out for a final pint and got to the door just as Colin was remembering to unlock it at noon. The Marvin Hagler guy was there, standing next to me, a message from Fate that too much sentiment could be my undoing. You never tip a barman, so instead I gave Colin a bottle of wine. I had one for John, too, and he came around from the saloon bar to accept it. He said he'd put it in his landlord's basement, where it would have company. He wrote his name and the address of the pub on a slip of paper——John, Cellarman, The Fountain, Amwell and Inglebert Streets, London, EC 1, England. He shook my hand. Would we be coming back? Of course we would. We were always on our way back somewhere, even as arms, legs, bodies stumbled forward. Cheers, John. All the best.

Jumpers
at Kempton Park

 That winter in London, I went to the Kempton Park racecourse whenever I could. Kempton Park is in Sunbury-on-Thames, Middlesex, some fifteen miles west of the city. I always caught a special racecourse train at Waterloo Station. Sometimes classical music was playing through speakers at Waterloo, soaring up into the diesel-rich atmosphere, and it lent a cheery note to departure. The train ticket cost about three dollars and fifty cents. Ordinarily, the compartments on the train were half filled with decorous men who wore a punter's uniform of topcoat or raincoat and checked woolen cap. They had on ties, of course, because to the English a tie signifies moral purpose. A nation without ties is a lax nation, slightly reprehensible in the eyes of the world. The men did not speak to each other, on pain of death, unless they were old friends, in which case a polite conversation was conducted. Preferred topics were gardening, the weather, and Tory politics. Horses were seldom mentioned. Anybody attempting to pass a tip or otherwise break the meditative calm was a candidate for defenestration.

That's why Dorothy Wharton-Wheeler took me by surprise. She sat down opposite me on the train one cold and blustery afternoon and asked me, in a loud voice, which horse I liked in the first race. I told her that I was a bad person to ask, because I was new in the country and I didn't really know very much about what the English call jumping races, over hurdles or steeplechase fences. These races, taken collectively, constitute the National Hunt season, which runs from midsummer to spring. I had done some research into the history of jumping, I said, and I'd been to Kempton Park a few times, but I didn't feel qualified to offer an opinion about potential winners, since I had enough trouble spotting them at the flat-racing tracks I frequented in the States.

"I like Musso in the first," Mrs. Wharton-Wheeler said.

I nodded, and went back to reading my racing paper, the *Sporting Life*. This is a fascinating publication, quite different from the *Daily Racing Form*. It contains none of the dense statistical material that Americans need to assure themselves that the racing game is not as randomly determined as it often seems to be. The English, with their more highly evolved historical perspective, understand the essential fruitlessness of computer-based scheming, so the *Sporting Life* sets them a problem in interpretation rather than in mathematics. Its front page always features tabloid-style photographs of horses, along with punning headlines in bold type:

SANDY LOOKS HANDY
IT'S ME AGAIN CAN SURPRISE
BROWN CHAMBERLAIN IS NOT SO GREEN NOW

Inside, there are race cards, or programs, for all the courses where meetings are being held—at least two every afternoon. The meetings last for a day or two, and they take place at more than forty courses, in England, Wales, Scotland, and Ireland. The cards list the horses entered in each race, their ages, handicap weights, trainers, owners, and jockeys. The horses' past performances are described in totally subjective language. There are a few numbers scattered among the lists, but they are straightforward items, lacking the nuance of decimals, so I always made my selections on the basis of unquantifiable factors, like class, fitness, and a horse's appearance in the paddock.

According to the *Sporting Life,* Musso was favored in the first at Kempton Park, although he was expected to receive a strong challenge from Another Generation. I looked over at Mrs. Wharton-Wheeler. She was cleaning her glasses with a tissue. She wore a bulky sweater, a tweed skirt, and nononsense nurse shoes. Her hair was cut in a Dutch-boy bob.

"Have you been to Ascot yet?" she asked.

I told her that I'd been to Ascot once, in autumn, when the trees along the backstretch were still turning color, and that the races had had a wonderful pastoral quality about them—it was a bit like Thomas Hardy's novels, with the landscape in the ascendant. I said that I'd hoped to see the Queen at Ascot, or at least Julie Andrews, but I'd been disappointed.

"The Queen attends Royal Ascot," Mrs. Wharton-Wheeler said. "That's an entirely different sort of thing, isn't it? Upper crust and all that. It's the Queen Mother who loves jumping. She's got her own horses. Fulke Walwyn is her trainer."

Actually, I'd seen the Queen Mother once, at Newbury. She sat in a glassed-in box near the finish line to watch a horse of hers, Sindebele, run his first race ever. Sindebele fell down while trying to jump a hurdle.

Mrs. Wharton-Wheeler said that she'd visited twelve racecourses in her life, and she proceeded to recite them to me. Some of the courses were so obscure that their names sounded like the names of forgotten Elizabethan poets— Catterick, Plumpton, Taunton, Towcester. You could imagine these guys sitting at a tavern table and sharing a bottle of hock while couplets rattled around in their brains. Mrs. Wharton-Wheeler laughed at the analogy. She was a former secondary-school teacher, with a degree in literature, and she was familiar with the work of several American poets, including Robert Frost and Allen Ginsberg. A student had given her a copy of Ginsberg's *Howl,* back in the terrible sixties. It had not upset her, she said—nasty words were not so bothersome after you'd reached a certain age.

Mrs. Wharton-Wheeler told me that she lived in a suburb of London, with her husband, a retired building contractor, who had no interest in racing. "He was born in the city," she said. "He doesn't care for country things." For her, jumping races were a country thing. They reminded her of her childhood, in Devon. She could still remember standing on a hillside on Boxing Day many years ago and watching the local squires ride to hounds, over undulant farmland littered with obstacles—hedgerows, fences, streams. Jumping racecourses—especially those used for steeplechases—simulate these obstacles. Mrs. Wharton-Wheeler saw her first professional jumping race meeting when an uncle took her to Wincanton, in Somerset, just after her sixteenth birthday. It pleased her so much that she began going to jumping races at every opportunity. On her honeymoon, in Scotland, she dragged her husband to the racecourse at Ayr, and he had such an awful time that he vowed never to accompany her again. Since then, he has avoided racing as devoutly as Henchard, the Mayor of Casterbridge, avoided drink, so Mrs. Wharton-Wheeler always travels to the races alone. She survives, she said, by making friends.

Mrs. Wharton-Wheeler is an anomaly, for jumping has always been a gentleman's game. It has its roots in the races that eighteenth-century Irish squires used to hold to test the mettle of their hunting stock. Often, the squires chose a village church steeple to mark the finish line—hence the word "steeplechase." Today, owners of jumping horses need a noble dedication to the sport—and a bank account indifferent to downward fluctuations—in order to participate. Even at the largest courses, the average purse on an average day seldom amounts to more than two thousand dollars. Jumping is a small-scale endeavor, so the temptation to fiddle with horses or to run crippled or indisposed stock is greatly reduced. The laws governing medication are very strict. Anti-inflammatory drugs (like Butazolidin, which props up thousands of near-lame animals in the States) are forbidden, and so are steroids, Lasix for bleeders, and most other chemicals commonly found in a vet's bag.

Consequently, jumping horses look good: groomed to perfection, their shiny coats given a high gloss by the eternal damp that passes for winter weather in Britain. The original jumpers in Ireland had no thoroughbred blood, but practically all of today's jumpers are in a direct line of descent from the three thoroughbred foundation sires who were imported to England in the late-seventeenth and early-eighteenth centuries—the Byerly Turk and the Darley and Godolphin Arabians. The jumpers are often larger and burlier than other thoroughbreds, with broad chests and muscular hindquarters, which grant them the staying power necessary to complete grueling races that almost never cover less than two miles. They tend to mature rather slowly. The best steeplechasers are between eight and ten years old, and they may run in reasonably decent form until they are twelve or thirteen. Testaments to extreme longevity are not unusual. Mac Vidi, a stolid gelding with the genetic makeup of Bernard Baruch, is still touring courses at the age of sixteen.

Most jumping horses start out in races over hurdles, where the obstacles—brushy hedges about three and a half feet high—are lower and more resilient than the stiff fences that must be negotiated in steeplechases. The fences at Kempton Park are made of birchwood thatched over with gorse, an evergreen with yellow flowers that grows on moors and heaths; they do not yield to pressure, as hurdles do. A horse that clips a fence with its heels, or jumps too early or too late, or bridles at the severity of the challenge is generally guaranteed to fall. The falls are miserable to watch. Jockeys float into the air, then hit the ground with a bone-cracking thud. If they're lucky, their mounts don't land on top of them. Horses come down in an awkward tangle of limbs, but surprisingly few of them are hurt so badly that they have to be destroyed. An inordinate number rise quickly to their feet, shake themselves, and take off again in riderless pursuit of the pack, providing yet another obstacle in the race. It's the jockeys who seem to suffer most; broken collarbones are a dime a dozen, and so are broken arms and legs.

Ever since the inception of steeplechasing, there have been outcries about its supposed brutality. One of the sport's most vehement early opponents was Charles Apperly, known pseudonymously as Nimrod, who wrote about fox-hunting for magazines. It was said of Nimrod that he was always trying to make six words do the work of two. In 1839, he sent an open letter to both the *Times* and the *Standard* in an effort to alert the public to the horrors of steeplechasing, but the letter was never printed—because, according to Nimrod, the person charged with delivering it to London disapproved of its contents and burned it. Nimrod did manage, before his death, in 1843, to write about the plight of Grimaldi, a much admired horse whose heart had burst after a steeplechase at St. Albans. He informed his readers that Dr. Wardrop, a noted surgeon, had examined Grimaldi's heart and had found it to be "of uncommon dimensions, larger than that of Eclipse, but it could not stand steeplechasing," and "it burst in the moment of victory."

An unidentified friend of Nimrod's was even more vociferous in his objections to steeplechasing. "I boldly affirm that it is no criterion of the best horse but a mere game of chance and gambling transaction," this fellow wrote, in a letter that did get published. "From many quiet and observant farmers I heard the following remark, 'This is a cruel exhibition, with not one feature to recommend it . . . and if the good sense of Englishmen does not put it down, I hope the Legislature will.' " In response to such ongoing complaints, the Grand National Steeplechase Hunt Committee was formed, in 1866, to govern the affairs of the sport. Most of the committee's members were also members of the prestigious Jockey Club, and over the years they adopted a stringent body of rules designed to keep mishaps to a minimum. But mishaps will always be part of jumping. It is high-risk racing, exhilarating to watch, and that is one reason that Mrs. Wharton-Wheeler returns to the racecourse again and again.

Another reason is that Mrs. Wharton-Wheeler loves horses. "I have a strong feeling for animals," she told me. This does not make her unique in Britain; the English adore their pets. The best-selling author Barbara Woodhouse has a TV show on the BBC called "Barbara's World of Horses and Ponies." Barbara trains the horses and ponies by blowing up their noses. I think she may have learned this from an Indian tribe in Argentina. She had another show during which she visited viewers' homes and gave them advice about their problem dogs. Once, I saw her admonish a slow-moving dog by shaking a plastic bag at it. She even did a special show in Beverly Hills, where she dropped in on celebrities and met their pets. Some of the celebrities were Britt Ekland, Wilfrid Hyde-White, David Soul, and Zsa Zsa Gabor. During the special, Barbara confessed to William Shatner that she knew that when she got to Heaven she'd be reunited with her own dog, who'd died some years before.

When Mrs. Wharton-Wheeler and I got off the train at Kempton Park, it was less cold outside than it had been in London. A little sunlight was leaking through the haze. This is known in England as "a bright interval." Ahead of us I could see the main grandstand. It is an imposing brick structure, with the fortress-like look of the nineteenth-century churches, office buildings, and row houses you see all over London. This is orderly architecture, built to withstand the elements and outlast any of its inhabitants. It inspires an inescapable reverence for the past; indeed, nothing in Britain is as sacrosanct as what happened yesterday.

The original Kempton Manor was owned by Robert, Earl of Mortain. It was mentioned in the Domesday Book, of 1086. Later, the manor was acquired by the Crown, and it remained in royal hands until the Tudor era. In the thirteenth century, Henry III built a hunting lodge there and stocked the woods with deer. The early Plantagenet kings visited Kempton Manor, usually when traveling from Westminster to Windsor, and they probably did some hunting. But the lodge eventually fell into disrepair, and it was dismantled in 1374. Some years later, Elizabeth I leased the manor to William Killigrewe. It was the home of a succession of country gentlemen until S. H. Hyde—a solicitor, a Tory, and a racing buff—acquired the property in the 1870s and worked a transformation.

Admission to Kempton Park is very dear, in line with an inflated economy. The cheapest grandstand enclosure, known as the Silver Ring, confines punters to a macadam area almost a half mile from the winning post. It costs three dollars to enter. There is nothing silvery about the Silver Ring. Being there is more like being in purdah, with a veil drawn over your eyes. Mrs. Wharton-Wheeler and I paid about eight dollars apiece to get into Tattersall's, the middle enclosure—named for Richard Tattersall, who founded one of the first British bloodstock firms, in 1766. The Members' enclosure, right next to Tattersall's, is open to non-members willing to part with thirteen dollars. I had spent the thirteen once, just to see who was over there. They looked to me like a bunch of people who were drinking hard in order to forget that they'd overextended themselves in financial matters. Bottles of champagne were making the rounds, and there was a good deal of clubby chitchat going on. The men called each other Nigel or Basil. They had velvet collars on their topcoats and raincoats. Their hats were brown felt, with little snap brims. A few of them had brought their wives along, and the wives sat in clutches at Formica tables in various bars, smoking slow cigarettes and projecting an air of stylish indifference that they must have cultivated at ten thousand boring cocktail parties over the years.

I told Mrs. Wharton-Wheeler that at American tracks the class divisions are made vertically. You rise to the top, but the masses are always around you, so that you can't forget your humble origins. The American grandstand represents a society in flux, with certain dreams of upward mobility intact. In Britain, the division in grandstands is horizontal. There is no chance that a Member will ever be reduced to the Silver Ring, and no chance that a Silver Ringer will ever arrive at Member status. Mrs. Wharton-Wheeler said that that was all very well, but she was getting hungry, and she was going to eat her sandwich and hard-boiled egg at the parade ring—the paddock.

I hadn't carried my lunch with me, so I went to the Winners' Bar, on the ground level of Tattersall's, and ordered a light ale and a pork pie. The pork pie was very heavy. It was only two or three inches in diameter, but I had trouble lifting it to my mouth. This was a pork pie that could have been flung from a catapult at the Visigoths. It tasted all right, though, and I preferred it to the cellophane-wrapped cheese rolls available at another bar, upstairs. You could buy a hamburger upstairs, too. It came in a Styrofoam container, just like the burgers at McDonald's, but you had to chew it for a long time before it disassembled. At Newbury once, I'd bought a fine pre-race meal from a fishmonger who sold cockles, mussels, whelks, and jellied eels from a cart. He served his delicate offerings in fluted paper cups, and you ate them with a splash of hot sauce, sucking in the essence of the sea.

After I'd eaten, I joined Mrs. Wharton-Wheeler at the parade ring. It's a fenced-in oval behind the grandstand, with a path on its periphery, over which horses are walked in preparation for a race. Just outside the fence, there are seats of a sort—round, padded cushions covered with black vinyl, each of which is attached to a thin metal leg driven into the ground. The seats are so small that an average-size haunch necessarily overlaps into space, but they afford you a fine proximity to the animals. We could almost reach out and touch Musso when he passed by. The sardine effect that can make American paddock-going so hazardous rarely comes about at Kempton Park, even when six or seven thousand people—a big crowd for jumping—are in attendance. The extreme courtesy that prevails everywhere in Britain is evident at the parade ring. Nobody pushes, nobody shoves, nobody threatens to use your ear as an ashtray. You can watch the horses at your leisure, thinking your usual deep and revelatory thoughts.

"There's John Francome," Mrs. Wharton-Wheeler said, nodding in the direction of a sinewy-looking jockey who had come into the parade ring and now stood next to Musso. I had seen Francome ride before. He has an uncanny ability to get the most out of his mounts, combining strength with gentleness. Sometimes he seems to lift faltering animals over fences; sometimes he seems to bind them together when their legs go wobbly after a jump. Currently, he is a leading rider in jumping races, and everybody thinks that he is good enough to earn himself a place in the history of the sport.

The first great jump jockey was one Captain Becher, a commissioned officer in the Buckinghamshire Yeomanry early in the nineteenth century. As a child, Becher had been forbidden by his father to ride donkeys, on the assumption that such low animals would spoil any talent he might have for handling horses. Becher's chief patron was Thomas Coleman, a steeplechase entrepreneur who had bought the Chequers Tavern in St. Albans and turned it into the Turf Hotel. Becher lived at the hotel, and for a time he rode only Coleman's stock, but by 1829, he was traveling all over England to accept mounts. He was known for his riding skills, and also for parlor tricks he performed at post-race social gatherings. Becher could run around a room on the wainscoting without ever touching the floor. He could kick the ceiling. He could imitate the noises made by chickens, goats, ducks, and cows. It was Becher who rode Grimaldi in that fateful St. Albans steeplechase. He was so fond of Grimaldi that he obtained one of the horse's forelegs as a souvenir. He liked to show it off to friends. He had his last public ride at Doncaster in 1847. Later, he was given a sinecure as Inspector of Sacks on the Great Northern Railway in Lincolnshire. He died in 1864, at the age of sixty-seven, and his possessions were sold at auction—lathe, tool chest, fish can, grindstone, scarlet hunting coat, velvet caps, driving whips, racing saddle, and seven silk jackets. "These seven," said the auctioneer, "have seen many a flourishing day."

Dick Francis, whose thrillers often have a racing background, was a professional jump jockey for almost ten years, and he has recounted his adventures in an autobiography, *The Sport of Queens.* They give some indication of the vagaries of a jump jockey's life. Early in Francis's career, at a small rural meeting, he rode a horse that unseated him, then bolted from the track, galloped into a stream, and swam away. Francis rode a doped horse once. The animal was so cranked up that it ran right through the first hurdle, throwing Francis, and veered off into the woods nearby, where it was finally captured hours later. In 1956, Francis rode Devon Loch, the Queen Mother's horse, in steeplechasing's most famous event—the Grand National, at Aintree. Devon Loch jumped all thirty fences with ease, and he was far ahead going into the stretch, and then suddenly and mysteriously went spread-eagled fifty yards before the winning post. "That's racing, I suppose," the Queen Mother later said. The youngest Francis, a three-year-old, invented a new game to play around the house. "I'm Devon Loch!" the boy would cry, falling to the floor. "Down I go, bump!"

Francis enjoyed the freedom of being a jump jockey. He had to commute to courses throughout the country, often in treacherous weather, but he claims not to have minded. He understands how fortunate he was to be successful; only one in forty jump jockeys makes the job pay. Francis's attitude toward accidents is cavalier: "The number of bones each jockey may expect to break varies a great deal, because some men have strong bones, and others brittle." Francis cracked a leg or two every season. He broke his collarbone twelve times, but he was not as fragile as Jack Dowdeswell, a rider whose collarbone shattered as readily as crystal. Dowdeswell's collarbone was ultimately removed and replaced by an artificial one. Francis never severed his spinal cord, like Lionel Vick, or broke his back, like Fred Winter. Francis says that a jump jockey has about one chance in five hundred of being killed, and that this is a death rate very much lower than the rate for window cleaners. "If any window cleaners' wives are reading this," Francis writes, "I sincerely apologise for passing on this unwelcome piece of news."

Other jockeys had joined Francome in the parade ring. They were busy checking their tack—adjusting stirrups and tightening girths—while making the obligatory small talk with owners. They had a cocky assurance about them. There were no foreigners among them, so the racial tension that sometimes exists among jockeys in the States was absent. Unlike the abnormally diminutive riders who work the flats, they had not been forced into their profession by any freak of nature. Some of them had simply grown too heavy for flat racing—jumping horses carry an enormous amount of weight compared to sprinters—and some of them had never wanted to be anything but jump jockeys. They stood between five feet six and five feet ten, and they weighed between a hundred and forty and a hundred and sixty pounds. They had wiry builds, complemented by strong backs and shoulders, which they'd developed while holding on to rogue horses who pulled hard at the reins. The torsos of older riders—men in their forties—seemed as stretched as taffy. They prided themselves on their horsemanship, but they were often criticized by experts for not knowing how to ride a race. Tactical brilliance is something best learned on the flat, where the pace of the race is fast, and the margin for error is slim.

Mrs. Wharton-Wheeler had circled John Francome's name on her race card. She had underlined Musso's name. She had put an asterisk next to the horse's number.

"There," she said, almost with a sigh. "I think I'm ready to make my bet."

The first person to make a book is said to have been a Lancashire man named Ogden, who stood up at the Newmarket races in about 1795 and quoted odds for all the horses running. Odgen was ridiculed and shouted down, but his idea took hold, and before long bookies were a fixture at every race meeting. At Kempton Park, about sixty of them set up shop on the macadam that separates Tattersall's and the Silver Ring from the racecourse proper. They are not permitted into the Members' enclosure. Members must transgress class lines to bet—with Bennie Edwards or George Fletcher, say, who are themselves members of an exclusive club, the Bookmakers' Association of Wales. The bookies pay a fee to the racecourse for their daily permit, but their spots, or pitches, are allocated internally on a strict seniority basis. A good pitch——close to the grandstand, easily accessible to punters——is handed down from father to son. Only the guttering out of a bookmaking dynasty will make a choice position available.

As much as is humanly possible, the bookies conform to a physical type. It is difficult to find a young bookie, for instance, or a thin bookie. Bookies seem to arrive at the racecourse in full-blown middle age, with solid, well-fed figures protected from the winter chill by raincoats or topcoats. They wear ties, of course, and also hats. The bookies have ruddy faces, splotched here and there by exposure to inclement weather and the alcohol necessary to withstand it. Most of them don't drink during working hours, for fear of muddling their accounts, but short-tempered, hung-over bookies are not unusual and can be identified by the nastiness with which they conduct their business.

Punters who find the bookies intimidating go inside the grandstand and bet with the Tote. Established in 1928 by an Act of Parliament, the Tote is a government-run concession, supervised by the Horse Race Totalisator Board. It has pari-mutuel windows at every major racecourse. Much of the Tote's daily take is ultimately returned to the people who own racecourses in the form of subsidies and purse monies. Like other government operations, the Tote has suffered from mismanagement, including some creative accounting practices, which erupted in a "Totegate" scandal.

Mrs. Wharton-Wheeler never bets with the Tote. "I don't like all that machinery," she told me as we wandered among the bookies. This was a novel objection. Most punters dislike the Tote because its odds fluctuate—like the odds at American tracks—depending on the amount of money bet on each horse. If you bet with a bookie, the odds of the wager are fixed, no matter what happens in the future. But Mrs. Wharton-Wheeler was more interested in the quality of the exchange than in whatever edge it might bring her. She was looking not for the best price available on Musso—the prices offered ranged from six to four to two to one—but for Eddie Martin, her favorite bookie. "It's a bit like a street market, don't you think?" she asked. I agreed. The bookies could have been selling shoes or sealing wax. They chanted their odds in rich, raw voices, forming a cockney choir.

While Mrs. Wharton-Wheeler went off in seach of Martin, I watched a bookie named Fred Binns work. Binns cuts a flamboyant figure, with the look of the aging aviator about him. In fact, during the war, he was a pilot. Like the other bookies, he stood on a small wooden platform that allowed him to see over the heads of the crowd. The platform also gave him a quite literal elevated status that caused waffling bettors to tremble a little. Next to Binns was a tripod from which a slate was hung. A sheet of tissue-thin paper printed with a list of the horses entered in the first race covered three-quarters of the slate, leaving a column at the left unobscured. In the column, Binns chalked the odds he was offering. The prices changed often, depending on the sway of the action, and Binns kept wiping out numbers and making corrections. When he accepted a bet, he tossed the money into a leather bag hanging from the tripod, then shouted the terms of the wager to his clerk, who stood behind the tripod and recorded the transaction in a ledger. There was something of Scrooge and Cratchit in the byplay. "Eight-eight-two," Binns might say as he handed a bettor a ticket bearing that number. "Five pounds on Musso at seven to four." The ticket was the bettor's receipt: a white cardboard rectangle with orange stripes, busy and post-modern in design, that was embellished with Binns's name, his credentials, some mysterious letters, and a code word—"Miss Binki." The bookies had new tickets printed every few days, always with a new code word, to protect themselves from counterfeiters. Jack Cohen's code word that day was "Officer Kelly"; Steve Dee's was "Tom Horn."

I had been doing surprisingly well at the jumping races. I thought they were easier to handicap than the flat races back home, in spite of the lack of statistics. Usually, there are only two or three serious contenders in any race—except for major events, when all the best eligible horses show up. You have another advantage in that the jumping game is dominated by a handful of trainers. Whenever they run a horse, you know that the horse is fit and has a shot at winning. The problem is that other punters have the same information, so it's hard to find a reasonable price on most favorites. The favorite wins in forty-one per cent of all steeplechases and in thirty-nine per cent of all hurdles, and this means that you are often forced to take very short odds on the horse you like. I took Musso at six to four from Sol Parker, a bulldog-faced man with a snappish demeanor. " 'E's not in a bad mood," said a cockney gent who was hanging around Parker's pitch. "It's just 'is nature."

The Kempton Park circuit is roughly triangular and about thirteen furlongs long. It has three courses, of natural turf, laid out side by side: the ste .echase course; the hurdles course; and an unimpeded course, used for flat racing, in season. The infield has a pond and an old-fashioned, non-electronic tote-board. Musso's race would cover about two-and-a-half miles, over hurdles. The horses would go around the course about one-and-a-half times, and would make ten jumps. I watched the race with Mrs. Wharton-Wheeler. The only seats in the grandstand are on the top level, so we stood with other punters on its concrete steps, which provide the main viewing area. The horses were milling about in the distance, way out on the backstretch, waiting for the starter to release them. There is no starting gate in jumping races. The riders position their mounts where they want them and take off at a modest gallop when they get the signal. The action sneaks up on you—no bells, no yammering announcer. Since the pace is slow, you are drawn in rather gradually. The stimulation is cerebral, without the sudden charge of adrenaline you feel when a six-furlong flat race begins.

Mrs. Wharton-Wheeler had binoculars, and she gave me a commentary on the running. "That chestnut colt is going well," she said, referring to Another Generation, who had the lead. Another Generation, being a colt, was a rarity. Most jumping horses are geldings, because the obstacles they must jump pose a constant threat to the genitalia. Gelding makes them worthless at stud, of course, but it has a wonderful effect on the sport, since owners keep their horses performing instead of retiring them early. When the horses passed the grandstand for the first time, I was impressed by how easily they seemed to take to the turf. They had been trained on farms, and the grass probably had a pleasing familiarity to them.

The horses continued around, into their second circuit. Several of them were beginning to tire, and it showed in their jumping: more often than not, they brushed the hurdles with their bellies as they went over them. As the horses approached the stretch—called the run-in—it became clear that Musso and Another Generation would battle each other to the wire. They drew away from the others by five or six lengths. Such a large gap is not unusual in jumping races, because the races are a test of endurance more than anything else. Francome applied some of his special urging, and Musso responded by pulling ahead and taking the race by a neck.

Mrs. Wharton-Wheeler was very happy. She squeezed my arm. She'd bet a pound with Eddie Martin, and now that pound was two. Sol Parker would have to make my three pounds worth almost seven. Mrs. Wharton-Wheeler and I were handicapping geniuses. We congratulated each other. Mrs. Wharton-Wheeler suggested, rather tentatively, that we pool our winnings and go for broke on the next race. Then she said no, that wasn't fair, because I'd won more than she had. I said that I didn't care, since I was an American, and Americans were supposed to be reckless with their money. She told me that she'd had an American friend who gave her cigarettes during the Second World War. I told her that every person I'd met in England had had a friend like that.

We went to the parade ring and agreed to play Fire Drill, another favorite. Fire Drill was to be ridden by Steve Smith-Eccles. I thought this was a good sign, because Smith-Eccles had two last names, like Mrs. Wharton-Wheeler. I passed four pounds to Les Nicholls, accepting odds of seven to four. Fire Drill ran well for a while, but then he hit a steeplechase fence and fell. Mrs. Wharton-Wheeler was devastated. She felt that she'd led me astray. I told her that that wasn't possible—I'd strayed long before.

I convinced her that we should try again. We put two pounds apiece on Sweeping Along, a big, strapping horse who had run a good second at Newbury last time out. The race was the longest of the day—a steeplechase of about three miles. The horses had to make almost two complete circuits, jumping each obstacle on the course—with the exception of one puddle about twelve feet wide—twice. This added up to fourteen plain fences and four fences with six-foot-wide open ditches behind them. The usual time of a three-mile chase is about six minutes, so your mind tends to wander a bit, just as it does in Hardy novels when Hardy suspends his plot to offer a disquisition on Wessex. Characters are set in motion, but the landscape dominates them. I was watching mallards on the infield pond when I felt Mrs. Wharton-Wheeler squeezing my arm again. Sweeping Along had been trailing the field, but now he was in overdrive, jumping fences with aplomb. He was fully in command when he reached the last one, and he jumped it as if he had wings.

We celebrated our victory by retiring to the Winners' Bar and ordering bottles of Guinness. Mrs. Wharton-Wheeler insisted that we sit at the back of the room, far away from the food counter, where a tempting steak-and-kidney pie was resting on a sideboard. She was on a diet, she said. She had been on the diet since 1978, and she didn't think she'd ever get off it. I asked her if she was planning to go to Ascot later that week. She said that she wanted to, but that, really, going to the jump races was an expensive proposition, and she had to exercise some control.

I couldn't argue with her. An afternoon at Kempton Park—including racing paper, train ticket, admission, lunch, and drinks—put you about twenty dollars out of pocket before you'd even made a wager. This was about double the cost of an afternoon at an American track, but you got far better quality racing for your money. The horses were not drugged or crippled, and the racecourse management wasn't always trying to manipulate you. If you bought a wedge of steak-and-kidney pie, you tasted real steak and kidneys; I'd eaten so many plastoid pizzas at tracks in the States that my body was probably permanently damaged. But you couldn't blame the racecourses for charging so much—not when the gambling action was controlled by the bookies and the government. They were hurt by television, too. Most major races are shown on TV, so a lot of people stay at home to watch them, or go to the local pub, making their wagers at one of the twelve thousand betting shops around. I'd read somewhere that quite a few of the courses were in financial trouble, and I hoped that somebody would devise a plan to help support them. It seemed to me that jump racing was a sort of museum piece, small-scale and rather pure in its intentions, and that it ought to be preserved, in one form or another, so that the slowed-down, country way of life it represented would continue to be available. The races made you feel good, win or lose, and that was reason enough to care about what happened to them.

As we drank our Guinness, I asked Mrs. Wharton-Wheeler if she'd read much of Thomas Hardy.

"Almost all of him, I should think," she said. "Did you know that Devon is part of Hardy's Wessex? Well, it is. I used to use *Jude the Obscure* in some of my classes. That's such a sad book. Why is Hardy so sad, I wonder. Do you know the saddest thing in all of Hardy? It's when Tess and her brother have the accident with the mail cart. Her entire life changes after that. It gave me nightmares when I read it as a child. To think of a horse impaled on the shaft of a cart!"

We watched the sixth, and last, race of the afternoon down by the rail. The sound of the approaching horses was muted, like a bass drum wrapped in cotton. Every now and then, we could hear a horse's hooves clipping the top of a hedge. Neither of us had the winner, so we didn't have to wait around to collect. We walked back to the station through falling light that brought out the green in the winter grass and found an empty train compartment and settled in. Around us, the silent men tramped to seats and unbuttoned their topcoats or raincoats and began reading the evening paper. Mrs. Wharton-Wheeler and I exchanged addresses. I promised to send a copy of a new Ginsberg book when I got back to California, and she promised to study it carefully. She said that she would not be offended if Ginsberg still used nasty words. Then we talked some more about Hardy, and about Mrs. Wharton-Wheeler's reluctant husband. When we reached Waterloo, we stepped down onto the platform and shook hands. Mrs. Wharton-Wheeler's grip was very firm.

Tuscan Spring

The train from Rome to Florence passes through beautiful country. I rode it in March, after our long, cold winter in London. My wife was tired from traveling and had fallen asleep in her seat, so I bought a can of Peroni beer from a vendor, walked to the rear of the car, and looked out an observation window at vineyards and farms. Every now and then, a river came into view. It was high and muddy, carrying its spring payload of melted snow. I was considering whether or not I could afford to buy a fishing rod when a conductor in a neatly pressed uniform asked for my ticket. He did this casually, with the nonchalance that many Italians reserve for dispatching their duties. I asked him if there were trout in the river, and he said that of course there were trout. He spoke not like a fisherman but like a person who was proud of the rivers of Italy, certain that they could not be lacking in anything a tourist from America might desire.

"Are we in Tuscany yet?" I asked.

"No. Still Latium." He consulted a schedule of tariffs. "I'm sorry, *signore*, but you must pay a supplement for the *rapido*."

The rapido was the train we were on, the fastest in Italy.

It cost a bit more to ride than other trains. It rocked from side to side as it sped along the tracks. At first, the rocking was bothersome, but once you got used to it, it made you as secure and comfortable as a baby. My wife was not the only passenger it had put to sleep. I took some *lira* notes from my pocket. The notes were old. Several of them were held together with tape.

"Do you know what kind of grapes they grow here?" I asked.

"Nothing special."

"The wine from them is no good?"

"Non c'è male," he said, meaning "not so bad." "You can drink any wine when you're thirsty, but that won't make it *chianti.*"

I realized then that he must be Tuscan. There are some fine wines—Frascati, Colonna—produced in southern Latium, below Rome, but Tuscans don't like to admit it. For them, only chianti will do—preferably chianti from the rocky Classico district between Florence and Siena. The soil there is ancient clay-schist covered with flint, limestone, and pebbly sand. It is not duplicated anywhere else in Italy.

"Have you visited Florence before?" the conductor asked.

"Almost twenty years ago," I said. "I was a student there."

He nodded. "Many students in Florence. This time, will you stay?"

"If we can find a place to live."

"You will stay long?"

"Until the money runs out."

The conductor wrote something on his pad. "A restaurant," he said, handing me a piece of paper. "The best for eating. My cousin Angelo works there." I thanked him for the information. He smiled, gave me a mock salute, and moved on to the next car.

The vineyards and farms finally gave way to the outskirts of Florence. I saw two- and three-story apartment houses with small yards that contained the universal junk of the poor. The city looked cramped and inconsequential after the warm expansiveness of Rome. The people in the train station seemed to be trying to become invisible by drawing into themselves. They had none of the blatant narcissism of Romans, who treat Rome as an extension of their bodies, gliding through it at their ease.

We took a taxi to our *pensione* in the Santa Croce district. It was on the fourth floor of an old palace. The ceiling in the foyer had a mural of cherubim and seraphim blowing trumpets, but the rates were still cheap, less than thirty dollars a night. The manager was a slight, elegant, friendly man who had the impeccable manners of a true Florentine. In the crowded streets, these manners are often disguised, or transformed into brutal aggressiveness, but in the sanctity of a home—a good pensione is like a home—the graciousness of Florentines is manifest.

"Okay?" the manager asked, showing us a very clean room with two metal-frame cots like the cots you see in monasteries.

"Breakfast is included?"

"Of course," he said, sounding hurt.

I lay awake that night listening to the traffic and wondering if Florence would be able to live up to the version of it I'd imagined over the years. In my mind, it was a golden city, probably because I'd come to it when I was young and inexperienced, before I knew anything about suffering. Ever since my student days, I had wanted to return, but I'd never had the cash until quite recently, so I'd contented myself with talking schoolboy Italian to delicatessen clerks and staring at reproductions of Renaissance art in oversize books I borrowed from the library. The books were always missing a key plate, since anybody who has been touched by Italy is always trying to steal a piece of it. All around California there were stolen madonnas tacked up on apartment walls. I had a madonna on my bedroom wall, and also a print that I'd bought on that first trip—a Giotto fresco that shows some anguished monks gathered at the deathbed of St. Francis. The monks kiss his fingers and toes, they weep and moan, they throw their arms toward the sky in an outraged way. Now the fresco was just across the street from me, in the Church of Santa Croce, but I wasn't ready to look at it yet. I didn't want to be measuring things, making comparisons, not so soon.

Every morning, we ate breakfast in the dining room of the pensione. A maid in a blue housecoat brought us coffee and hot milk, fresh rolls, butter, marmalade, and packets of cherry jam. The manager always waved to us. He sat at a table by a window, feeding spoonfuls of sugar into his *espresso*. This is the Florentine vice—not sex or drink, but sugar, a palliative sweetness, a tiny secret on the tongue. I would linger awhile to read the daily paper in hopes of finding a short-term rental, but none were ever advertised. The Italian government has enacted strict rent control laws, and vacanoies are rare, except in summer, when people escape the heat by going to the seashore.

A friend in the States had given me the name of a woman who knew about things—real estate things. When I phoned her, she told me that she did not in fact know of anything in the city proper, but that there was a villa to rent in Arcetri, a hilly suburb south of Florence, a few miles from the Arno River. We went to look at it the next evening. It belonged to an elderly Austrian couple, but they were out of the country. A Swiss hotelier took care of it for them, because it was on his property—about three acres that formed a compound behind walls and fences.

The hotelier was generous, soft-spoken, with a polyglot's sensitivity to nuance. He led us downhill from his own house through a field strewn with wildflowers. In the distance we could see the villa—a boxy, three-story structure with a fieldstone exterior. The stones were tan and light gray, set off by brown window shutters. Olive trees were planted around the villa, along with cypresses and fruit trees. The rooms inside were furnished with heavy pieces in oak and mahogany. There was a stale fragrance of inoccupancy, of dust and history. The hotelier told us we could have the place for five hundred dollars a month, half the usual price, since it was not yet the season for tourism, and, besides, the house needed some repairs.

Almost as soon as we moved in, the repairs began to reveal themselves: The tiles on the terrace off the master bedroom were broken, and so was the furnace, and so were two of the four burners on the stove, and so was the oven in the stove. The wooden angel in the guest bedroom had two broken wings. The oil paintings in the living room, a cardinal and a madonna, had scratches and tears. The 1950s hi-fi console didn't work, and the television set worked only intermittently. The fireplace flue was broken. Several volumes of the complete Thomas Mann, in German, had suffered water damage and seemed about to burst with immemorial prose. The five bathrooms were in fair shape, but three of the six escritoires were wobbly. The door that was supposed to open from the third-floor study onto another terrace was stuck, so we had to climb out a window if we wanted to take in the view.

I must have climbed out the window about a dozen times while we were there, and my wife climbed out it once, on a warm, sunny, brilliantly clear afternoon just after we'd arrived. We sat together not on the terrace but on the orange-brown ceramic tiles of the roof. There were hundreds of bees buzzing around the lavender blossoms on our rosemary bushes. The olive trees were silvery green, almost iridescent. The cypresses among them had the stern, dignified presence of sentinels. All the wildflowers were open, a sea of color in waving grass. Beyond them, on the city plain, the buildings of Florence stretched out in shades of yellow ocher toward the mountains. If you can picture that moment, and how it pierced us, then you will understand how we were able to live quite happily in the villa all that spring without ever being troubled by its many imperfections, thinking what a fine bargain we'd got.

・　・　・

Arcetri is a quiet district of narrow, winding streets and lush vegetation. Almost every lane and path discloses a panoramic view, and that's part of the reason why Florentines think so highly of it. Many of them prefer it to Fiesole, the more famous hill to the north. Arcetri is closer to the *centro*, the city center, less rugged and agricultural. In Fiesole, you still get hints of wildness and mystery, of something inexpungibly weird, but Arcetri has been tamed. You can go for weeks without seeing a trace of animal life—no deer, no rabbits, no squirrels. The birds in the fields are common and domestic—blackbirds, sparrows, chickadees, pigeons. There are still vineyards and olive groves, but a few of them are rank and untended, marking a change from the old days in Tuscany, when nothing was ever wasted. Florentines ignore such faults and value Arcetri for its beauty and silence, for its fresh air. *"Ah, aria fresca,"* they say whenever the hill is mentioned, gesturing with their arms to show how the gentle breezes blow. On Sundays, after Mass and a big meal, they drive up to Arcetri from the smog-laden centro and stroll along Pian dei Giullari, the district's main street, taking in the sunshine, the leaves, and breathing deeply.

Although there are a handful of cottages and apartments in Arcetri, villas are the primary dwelling unit. The word "villa" simply means a house with a plot of land, but in Tuscany it also carries a connotation of "country place." Florentines did not start building villas in the countryside until the fourteenth century. Before then, the hills were the province of robbers, murderers, and renegade soldiers from various warring communes. Wealthy citizens were safer in town, behind locked gates and the walls of the city. The

Florentine police were very efficient. They imposed a curfew at sunset, and nocturnal crime was rare. Florence was the fifth most populous city in Europe at the time—larger than London, Athens, or Munich. According to the chronicle of Giovanni Villani for 1338, more than a hundred thousand people were jammed in among the damp stones and filthy running gutters. They formed an excellent culture for the breeding of infectious diseases, like the plague. The Black Death struck Florence in 1348 and killed off about forty thousand souls, but it was unique only in its numbers. Other plagues had preceded it, and others would follow, on the average of once every decade. Areas like Arcetri and Fiesole became increasingly attractive as an escape from contagion and social unrest.

Early villas in Arcetri resembled fortresses. Their towers and battlements were functional, and so were the strategic hillside sites on which families liked to build. Gradually, the need for protection decreased, and architects had more freedom to experiment. They began to evolve the basic design that you still find throughout Tuscany—plaster walls almost three feet thick, a tile roof, high-beamed ceilings, and red-brick floors. Leon Battista Alberti, who wrote a classic treatise on architecture during the *Quattrocento*, offered a detailed analysis of villa construction, down to minutiae, including the wine cellar. It ought to face north, he said, so that the tramontane winds would ventilate it and keep the wine casks dry. Alberti also praised the educational properties of a villa, its capacity for moral suasion. He believed that it was a wonderful place to bring up children, because they worked and played in the sun and grew up stronger than children who were left to languish in the city shade. For adults, a villa was a sanctuary from the evils that were always brewing in Florence. "You can hide yourself to avoid seeing . . . the great quantity of wicked mankind," Alberti said.

The best seasons to be "in villa" were spring and fall, when the weather was neither too hot nor too cold. Villa life was a contemplative affair, involving study, meditation, learned conversation, and long healthy walks. Florentines at their pastoral leisure played chess and other board games. They strummed lutes and sang popular songs. They watched fish swimming in ponds and streams. They sat in gardens. They kicked around soccer balls. They read Pliny and Cicero, and composed epigrams, ballads, and elegiac verses. They talked to nightingales. Sometimes there was a party with food and wine and dancing, and perhaps a lecture by a renowned scholar, but most villa residents were satisfied with their isolation, since they did plenty of socializing in the city. A notable exception was Niccolò Machiavelli, who lived in exile at San Casciano. He thought the countryside was dumb, tedious, positively rural. He called his farmhouse L'Albergaccio, "The Wretched Hotel," and said that he had nothing better to do than to indulge in games of cards and backgammon with a butcher, a miller, two bakers, and the innkeeper at his local inn. "Thus wrapped up with these fleas," he wrote, "my brain is steeped with mold. . . ."

We had trouble settling into the villa. Ten rooms, five baths—all the space and grandeur intimidated us. Ordinary conversations of married life turned into shouting matches.

"Where are you?"

"Here."

"Where?"

"*Here!*"

Too many echoes, too many potential ghosts. I think it helped us most to work in the kitchen—a small kitchen, meant for a maid—washing the pots and pans and making a list of necessary provisions. Food tends to center a person, to serve as a point of reference. We had no car, so we rode a rickety old bus from Pian dei Giullari down to the city to buy what we needed. Again, there were the views, the hazy air, the muted golds and yellows. Our shopping was parceled out among several merchants—one for produce, one for fish, one for poultry, one for staples. Everything was expensive, except for the most basic items—bread, coffee—whose prices are controlled by the government.

We bought bottles of extra virgin olive oil pressed not far from Piazzale Michelangelo. It was thick, dark green, redolent of olives. When it coated lettuce leaves or thin slices of fennel, it elevated them from the rank of mere vegetables into the realm of gastronomy. Tuscan cuisine is based on just such transfigurations of the patently simple. A new artichoke is nothing special if you steam it and eat it with lemon butter, but if you break off the raw leaves and dip them in *pinzimonio*—olive oil, coarse salt, freshly ground pepper—you discover subtleties you've never tasted before. The same is true of fava beans. In season, bowls of them are available in every *trattoria*. You grab a bunch of pods, split the seams with a nail, then dip the beans in sauce and pop them into your mouth, one by one. Each seed strikes the palate like a revelation.

Our wine merchant was a shy man with prematurely gray

hair. He wore a gray smock. Two gray cats were always prowling his shelves. They ate from his hand. The scene in the store reminded me of Yeats's account of Ezra Pound feeding the cats of Rapallo, taking bones and pieces of meat from his pocket. "He knows all their histories," said Yeats. The merchant sold us chianti classico in plastic-covered flasks. (Tuscans don't use straw so much anymore; it tends to rot.) The best flasks had three stars on their labels, beneath the black cock that serves as the classico logo.

The fish we bought were kept in a bin of crushed ice at the *pescheria*. We had snapper, shark, some type of bass. Once, we tried mullet. It was awful, the worst fish I've eaten anywhere. Mullet are bottom-feeders, muck-lovers. They ingest mouthfuls of mud, then sift through it for microscopic particles of animal or vegetable matter. That explains their flavor—muddy, with a soupçon of algae bloom. Better to stick to beef or chicken, or even rabbit. One of the produce ladies had a hutch in her backyard. If we ordered an execution on Thursday, we could pick up the dressed corpse on Friday morning. For those too faint of heart to give the necessary command, there are always sausages, including strongly scented links made of *cinghiale*, or wild boar. And there are all kinds of pasta:

anelli, or rings
anellini, little rings
anellini rigati, little grooved rings
cannellini, little reeds
cannelloni, big reeds
cappelli di prete, priests' hats
farfalle, butterflies

linguine, little tongues
maruzze, seashells
mostaccioli, little mustaches
penne, pens
stelle, stars
vermicelli, little worms
ziti, bridegrooms

A comprehensive list can be had from the Museo Storico degli Spaghetti—the Historical Museum of Spaghetti—in Pontedassio, near the Italian Riviera.

One morning when I was gathering wood to burn in our fireplace I met our neighbor, Signor Mancini, who lived with his wife in a cramped little cottage near the hotelier's house. Mancini was in his seventies, a tall, handsome, cheerful man who often wore a black beret. He had a garden that was about the size of a parking spot in any municipal garage. The residue of his winter crop was tossed onto the tilled earth, left to mulch into the soil—onion tops, cabbage leaves, decaying brussels sprouts. I watched him digging with a pitchfork, preparing the ground for some tomato plants he'd started in his greenhouse. He had an apron tied around his waist in the manner of a Tuscan *paesano*—somebody who'd been born and bred in the countryside and had been taught early on how to work in the fields with the most basic of tools.

We talked for a while, quite pleasantly, but then we reached a point beyond which we could not continue. There were limits to what I could say and understand. I felt bad about this, because it made Mancini impatient. He wanted to tell me things, *tried* to tell me things, and there I stood, as unresponsive as the wood in my arms. *"Ma, non so,"* he'd say, repeating the sentence in frustration—"I just don't know." I think he was relieved when I walked away. After this, we were always friendly when we met, discussing the weather or the price of food, but there was a tension beneath the interchanges. Mancini had the Tuscan peasant's contempt for anything frivolous. Instead of words, he gave me heads of lettuce from his garden, occasionally three at a time.

I had no problems communicating with Signora Mancini. She had no use for complexity. She was the hotelier's former maid, and she still did some housekeeping for a family on Pian dei Giullari. I'd run into her at the foot of the steep lane that led to our compound. She would wave, she would smile. "Buon giorno, signore!" she'd cry. Her voice was the voice of old Italian women in movies—the ones who survive. Her face was round, pretty, unscarred by expectations. Whenever she looked at me, she took all of me in without blinking. It was like being embraced, forgiven, a kind of nourishment. Signora Mancini trudged uphill. She was a happy soldier. She spoke of people, trees, old age, careless drivers who went ripping past. If I understood her, fine; if not, also fine. One afternoon as we were trudging along she found a blue plastic spaceman in the grass by the path. *"Tesoro,"* I said—a treasure. Signora Mancini thought this was the funniest thing she'd ever heard.

Sunday was family day for the Mancinis. I'd see them outside the cottage in their best clothes, waiting for the arrival of relatives, or for their daughter to drop off her only child—the *nipote*, the grandson. The boy was eight or nine. He had glasses and a homemade haircut—blondish hair, like a stranger from the north. He sat on the ground and played in the dirt, drawing pictures with a stick. The Mancinis sat in straight-backed chairs and watched the nipote run around, glad just to be near him. When the nipote went home at night, the Mancinis would go back to their ordinary routine, turning down the lamps in the cottage to save on electricity—this happens everywhere in Italy, an entire country reducing itself to a dull continental glow—and switching on the TV.

Sometimes after dinner, I fiddled with the TV in the villa and got it to work. The picture was in black-and-white, grainy, snowy, starring faintly transmitted figures who could have been beamed in from another planet. The shows I saw were simply conceived, with a premium placed on production values. I watched many *spettacoli*—multipart programs that often go on for weeks. The spettacoli feature singing, dancing, comedy routines, midgets in cars—the very essence of Milton Berlismo. Every *spettacolo* has a theme. I watched one called "What Do You Drink?" Each segment was devoted to a different beverage—wine, beer, vodka. In the beer segment, the dancers dressed like Germans. In the vodka segment, they dressed like Russians. The set remained the same.

I always tried to watch the two most popular shows in Italy, "Portobello" and "Flash." "Portobello" broadcasts live from various locations around the country. Its set is unique—about six spacious isolation booths with windows and telephones. Guests get to sit in the booths and take calls from the viewing public after they've told their story to the host, Enzo Tortora. A woman from Piacenza, say, might have invented a new kind of cheese grater and be in need of an investor. Some nuns from Abruzzi might want to sell their collection of Steuben glass to help the orphans. A lonely Milanese pharmacist might wish to meet and perhaps marry a nice woman, not too big. *Va bene,* all of you—get into the booths. While the phones ring, two men stripped to the waist sit down at a table for a wrist-wrestling contest. Maybe Enzo sings. Miracles are happening.

"Flash" is a quiz show with musical interludes. The host is Mike Buongiorno, a Roman with a perpetual tan and a lacquered look. Mike Buongiorno pronounces "Flash" as "Flesh." Every week, he asks a variety of questions—current events, films, politics—to three contestants. If a contestant is slow to answer, Mike Buongiorno teases him. "What's the matter, Corleone?" he might say. "You didn't sleep last night? You can't remember anything?" The winner of the preliminary round goes for the grand prize in a category of his own choosing. One champ, Mignini, was an expert in the history of the Ascoli soccer team. Mignini was about twenty. He dressed in knickers and hoped to become a movie star. He and Mike Buongiorno had an argument one night when they disagreed about a question's pertinence. Mignini said the question had nothing, *niente,* to do with Ascoli. Mike Buongiorno said that it did. Shortly after this, Mignini lost his title to a retired police officer, Gubellini. Gubellini's category of expertise was the life of Jesus.

. . .

Every day that spring, I took a long walk both for the exercise and the fresh air. Branches of wisteria trailed over the high walls along our lane, falling between shards of broken glass that had been set into the concrete to ward off thieves and terrorists. The lane joins Pian dei Giullari near the villa where Galileo had lived under house arrest after the Inquisition ordered him, in 1633, to recant his heliocentric theory of the universe. Just down from the villa is the only business in Arcetri—Omero, a restaurant. Omero used to be a classic Tuscan roadhouse offering an uncomplicated menu of regional specialties at modest prices, but it has been discovered, and the prices have gone up. The waiters dress in white shirts and black bow ties, and know how to intimidate tourists.

I liked to stop at Omero to have a glass of beer at the small delicatessen at the front of the restaurant. I liked the deli clerk, Alvaro, very much. Alvaro is a symmetrical person, firmly situated in time and space. A certain part of the community revolves around him. He was the *helios* of staples—wine, sugar, pasta, cold cuts. He always seemed to be preoccupied with a chronic complaint, either physical or metaphysical, and his behavior was never faked, so I was pleased whenever he chose to share a confidence or sell me a loaf of heavy, multigrain *integrale*—bread that he reserved for regular customers when it was in short supply.

If I was hungry for a snack, Alvaro would make me a sandwich. With a big bread knife, he'd slice the integrale thickly, then slap whatever I wanted between the slices.

"*Prosciutto?*" he'd ask, touching a perfectly cured haunch that dangled from the ceiling beams.

"Sì."

"Pecorino?" Pecorino is sheep's-milk cheese. It comes in three varieties. The oldest and driest, for grating, is what's known as pecorino Romano, or Romano cheese.

"Sì."

"Finocchiona?" A fatty Tuscan sausage that tastes of fennel.

"Sì."

Alvaro would smile, symmetrically. *"Si mangia bene."* One eats well.

The restaurant smelled of meat and poultry grilling over a wood fire. Alvaro turned the prosciutto haunches, turned the waxed balls of pecorino, seeking just the right amount of exposure for each. The waiters kept ducking into the deli for cigarettes. They'd defy their uniforms, becoming street-corner boys again, *ragazzi,* laughing and scratching themselves, discussing the girls inside.

Across from Omero is a working vineyard that's separated from the street by a low stone wall. I often sat on the wall and let the beer settle. Arcetri is not in the chianti zone, but the grapes in the vineyard were probably chianti grapes anyway—Sangiovese or Canaiolo, the wine's primary constituents. Vintners use Sangiovese for its body and alcohol. Canaiolo imparts a mellowness that tempers the bite of the wine without destroying it entirely.

The landscape in the vineyard resembled the landscape you find in the background of Renaissance paintings, where it shines in miniature, like a diamond seen through a keyhole. Artists could not bring it to the fore, of course, because they were locked into a system of patronage that demanded predominantly religious subject matter. The landscape was not well served when it did shift to center stage. You can see what happened to it if you go to the Gallery of Modern Art at the Pitti Palace. Painters blew it up in size and populated it with peasants they'd borrowed from Millet. The peasants toil and toil ceaselessly, in peasanty costumes, shouldering chubby infants who all have the same expression of weary resignation on their faces. How the infants learned to be resigned at just ten months of age is a mystery, but there is no mistaking the expression.

The worst aspect of these genre paintings is that they fail to capture the wonderful quality of Tuscan light you encounter in the countryside. This light—gold, yellow, always muted—has a tendency to soften the edges of things but not to deprive them of their actual rootedness in the world. Once you've been exposed to it, you'll notice it over and over again, in Ghirlandaio, in Fra Angelico, in almost every great artist of Tuscany. It is completely different from the hard blue marine light of Venice, which draws its strength from the Adriatic. Venetian light is as analytical in its way as the work of Giovanni Bellini, who could not have painted with such precise intensity if he'd been Florentine.

I usually ended my walks at Torre del Gallo, a nineteenth-century reconstruction of a medieval tower with battlements. Torre del Gallo looks like a fairy-tale castle, the sort of place where a hunchback ought to be ringing bells. Next to it is La Gallina, "The Hen," a ruined villa that once belonged to the Lanfredini family, ambassadors for Lorenzo de' Medici. I met a glassblower here one day, while I was leaning against the gate. He was old but fit, with lung power that he kept up by riding his bicycle through Arcetri. The hills were no obstacle to him, he said, although he sometimes had to pause to wipe his brow and say hello to a friend. No more glassblowing, he said, the industry's shot. *"Macchine, macchine."* Machines, machines.

The longer we lived in Arcetri, the more oppressive Florence began to seem. The city was distasteful, crowded. The air really wasn't fit to breathe. Twenty years ago, the expensive dress shops, the purveyors of truffle sandwiches and two-hundred-dollar shoes, were confined mostly to the area around Via Tornabuoni, near the centro, but now pockets of refinement jumped out from the old stones in unexpected districts, driving away the tripe sellers, the rag dealers, the men who sharpen knives on grinding wheels. Everywhere I saw boutiques, neon, shiny plate glass, the spacy mannequins of Giorgio Armani. I heard as much swooning over Missoni as over Masaccio. The statues in the Piazza della Signoria had become backdrops for tourist snapshots, a means of validating one's presence in a foreign land. The Grand Canyon, the Eiffel Tower, Michelangelo . . .

Somehow, the art that is the essence of Florence, its true reason for being, manages to withstand the various pressures put upon it. In the Uffizi, in the Bargello, in churches and chapels, I discovered that twenty years had taught me to see with my own eyes instead of the eyes of my teachers. Take Raphael, for instance. True, he was a great painter, but he was also a joker, always darting in and out of the frame, sending up his subjects. Look, he says, confiding, that fat, foolish, hypocritically pious man has paid me to paint his portrait, and he won't have the nerve to complain when I give him an image that shows every wart and pimple. This madonna, says Raphael, the one who's about to giggle?: I made love to her last night. Leonardo da Vinci pays no attention to his madonnas. He leaves them stranded, half finished, on insubstantial rocks. He's a dreamer, an eternal schoolboy with a gyroscope for a mind. It spins from one idea to another, never stopping—good-bye, girls, Leonardo's off to help some duke win a war.

Some of the most famous paintings in the Uffizi, including many Botticellis, had recently been restored. I found them hard to look at, because they were so different from what I'd come to think of as the "originals." The colors were bright, glowing, K-Mart clean. I thought they'd been tampered with, touched up, but I was wrong. Only dark coats of varnish, of soot and grime, had been removed. The man who takes care of this work for the museum, Umberto Baldini, made his name by supervising the restoration efforts that followed the terrible 1966 flood. His studio is at the Fortezza da Basso. Baldini is a sophisticated theoretician, a believer in the relevance of technology, but he has a profound respect for an artist's integrity. Any portion of a canvas or fresco that Baldini has restored must show the restoration, not hide it. (In the past, some restorers tried to improve upon the masters, adding details and brushstrokes, erasing one color to add another.) Baldini uses *colore neutro*—a blend of red, yellow, and blue—to patch the trouble spots. If the neutro is applied next to a strong red, the red in it becomes stronger; the same formula holds for yellow and blue.

One afternoon, I went to the Church of Santa Croce, to the Bardi Chapel, to visit Giotto's monks. The chapel was quiet, cool. Candles were burning. The monks were still mourning, still throwing their arms to the sky. I could remember that time, twenty years ago, when their grief had seemed exaggerated, even cute, but now I couldn't look at them without being reminded of my own irrevocable losses.

Florence was distasteful, yes, but it was still Florence. I couldn't avoid it for more than a day or two. I'd ride the bus to Ponte di San Niccolò, then walk the banks of the Arno, oblivious of traffic. Men sat on the banks, fishing with long poles—maybe thirteen or fourteen feet. The poles had no reels. The men caught ugly fish, mullet-cousins. I never saw any trout. If the fishing was slow, the men took slingshots from their pockets and scattered pellets of bait in the water.

My wife bought a leather purse at a shop near the Pitti Palace. The price was good. The man who'd made the purse was named Silvano. He was proud, a little irascible, definitely from the old school of Florentine craftsmen. To the strap of the purse, he attached a leather tag: *Made by hand, Silvano.*

Students from Italian high schools came to the city on their Easter break. They dressed with great panache, throwing together wardrobe items to create a lexicon of international teen. On the buses, they behaved abominably, pushing past old people and cripples, singing, causing scraps. Nobody ever scolded them. In Italy, children are sacred, forever indulged.

We learned the word *sciopero*. It means "strike."

There were several bus drivers' strikes. Often we didn't know about them, because there were several journalists' strikes when newspapers stopped publishing.

There was a big general strike.

Terrorists were active in the south. In Naples, they stole some diamond-tipped bullets from a government armory and used them to assassinate a high-ranking police official, shooting him through the bulletproof windows of his car.

We ate at a fine little restaurant, Da Noi, and had a *risotto* made with squid ink. It was so good that we ordered another version of it a week later at a fancier place. The cook substituted tomatoes, onions, and garlic for the squid. The dish was like Spanish rice. I complained to the manager. The manager said, "You think we have time to make a real risotto? Don't be absurd!"

We ate at a pizzeria where a dwarf was sitting on the back of a German shepherd.

The best place we ate was the trattoria that the train conductor had recommended. It was extremely busy, extremely cheap. The menu was handwritten, with many misspellings. It changed daily, depending on what was in season. The tables were pushed in one against another, jammed with Florentine grotesques. We shared ours with a gangly man in a black suit who did not speak to his two daughters during the meal. We had:

pappardelle sulla lepre, broad noodles with hare sauce
arselle, delicate clams steamed in stock
lombatine, grilled veal chops
spinach
mixed salad

pecorino and fruit
a liter of chianti
cappuccino

The bill, with service included, came to less than twenty dollars. Feeling expansive, I asked our waiter if he knew the conductor's cousin. The waiter had never heard of him, but the gangly man had. "Angelo?" he said. "Sure, I know him." Angelo'd had a fight with the boss and now he worked at another trattoria, across the river.

Suddenly, it was summer. The changeover had nothing to do with the calendar. The calendar said it was May, but the morning haze suddenly vanished, and it was hot all day long. Even Arcetri had smog. The wildflowers wilted, the ground wasn't damp anymore. I sat outside the villa, naked to the waist, like a wrist-wrestler, reading Italian poetry in translation. Salvatore Quasimodo. Eugenio Montale. Then Giuseppe Ungaretti, the son of Tuscan peasants who'd moved to Egypt and opened a bakery in Alexandria.

> *I know a city*
> *that every day fills to the brim with sunlight*
> *and in that instant everything is enchanted*

From Ungaretti, I went on to Henry David Thoreau. I took this as a sign of homesickness. Thoreau infuriated me one minute, then gripped me the next. He was an American, talking to himself, chanting truths he wanted to believe in.

I remember an afternoon late in the month when I walked through the field and stood among the olive trees and stared at the villa, not quite believing that I'd ever lived in it.

I phoned the woman who knew about real estate things and told her we'd be leaving in June. She had a client in mind for the villa, a painter who'd decided to leave his wife for the girl who'd been modeling for him since she was a child. The girl was a young woman now. I thought this was a fine story. I developed an elaborate fantasy about the model, her long shiny hair, her perfect complexion, her breasts, her legs, but when she came to see the house, she turned out to be round and totally suburban, with plans for redecoration in hand.

Florence, how you deceive!

The train station at Santa Maria Novella was swarming with people. The porter I hired to carry our bags tried to overcharge us. There was a mix-up about seats, and then an argument about something else. I was fed up with the rudeness, the clamor, glad to be leaving. I thought I'd never want to see Florence again, but then the train pulled away, and I recalled the afternoon when we'd sat on the roof of the villa, lost in glorious imperfection.

Sfida
at the Hippodrome

Ippodromo "Le Cascine," in Cascine Park, in Florence, would fit into the back pocket of any major racetrack in the States, but I still got very confused the first time I went out there. I caught the No. 38 bus on Pian dei Giullari. The bus wasn't very crowded, since it was two o'clock in the afternoon and almost everybody in Italy was eating or sleeping off the effects of having eaten. The only other passengers were a Dominican friar and the *pantaloni* man, who is legendary around the bus stop. He's about eighty years old, and he always has an elaborate bandage of gauze, cotton, and adhesive tape over one ear. He's known as the pantaloni man because whenever he sees a woman wearing pants of any kind he berates her for covering up her legs, which are a gift from God. Some people think the pantaloni man is crazy, but if so he's crazy like a fox. I never heard the friar speak to anybody, in all the times I saw him on the bus.

We had a pleasant ride down the hill, without any of the near-accidents that can enliven a No. 38 run. Pian dei Giullari is only as broad as an alley in some places, so if the bus driver is flirting with a girl or singing he has to apply the brakes rather quickly to keep from hitting the cars that come speeding up the hill. In Arcetri, the auto horn is essential equipment, and you get the feeling sometimes that a Klaxon should be attached to the hood of every Fiat. Riding a bus through the city center is not as dangerous, but it's often more frustrating because there are more obstacles to contend with—dogs, cats, daring pedestrians, horse carts, other buses, and the odd wandering chicken. Once, I was on a downtown bus that couldn't squeeze between two cars parked opposite each other on a ribbon of twelfth-century street. After we'd waited about ten minutes, stuck in the channel, three men got off the bus and carried the smaller car onto the sidewalk. Their return was greeted with applause.

The No. 38 dropped me at the Porta Romana, an old gate of the city which rises, stone by noble stone, to form a huge arch. There's always a great deal of automotive confusion around the arch; minor smashups involving major discussions are commonplace. One afternoon, I watched a crushed motorcycle explode, shooting flames into a sky already sulfurous with exhaust fumes and smoke from olive branches that had been pruned from trees and set to burning on the hillsides. Firemen arrived about a half hour after the explosion and sprayed chemicals on the ashes. They wore elaborate brown uniforms that made them look like gnomes from the Tyrol. Uniforms are even more popular in Italy than they are in America, perhaps because the country is even more desperately in need of leadership.

From the Porta Romana, I took a No. 13 bus across the Arno River to the eastern end of Cascine. The hippodrome was about a mile away, down a wide, tree-lined boulevard.

Cascine has none of the vastness of New York's Central Park, nor is it as lush and wild as Golden Gate, in San Francisco; instead, it's ineffably small-town, like a frame clipped from a Frank Capra movie, with lots of benches, picnics, bicycles, ice cream, and old dudes in hats and suspenders playing cards at folding tables set up in the leafy shade. There are plenty of familiar urban distractions around (noise, smog, dopers, prostitutes, a discotheque), but a fundamental innocence still manages to shine through. As I walked along, I had the sense that I was revisiting some place from my childhood, or from a childhood I had imagined. I bought a can of beer from a street vendor, who popped the top and stuck a straw through the opening. The vendor had cold sodas, too, and potato chips, and also a three-tiered lazy Susan on which he'd arranged little slivers of coconut. Water from a spigot at the top of the lazy Susan spilled over the slices, creating a miniature version of the tropics. Farther on, I passed a big, hairy-armed man who was carving rosemary-scented meat from the roasted carcass of a pig and stuffing generous portions into hard rolls. The pig's head was prominently displayed, like some symbol of the genuine.

The hippodrome proved to be built on the same intimate scale as Cascine. It has a small concrete grandstand that probably doesn't accommodate a crowd of more than a few thousand. Because admission is cheap (less than two dollars a ticket, except for special events), some patrons treat the hippodrome as an extension of the park, visiting it as they might the children's zoo or the curious monument to the Maharajah of Kolhapur, an Indian prince who was cremated in Cascine in 1870. I saw a surprising number of young mothers pushing along *bambini* in strollers, heading for a playground near the grandstand, where there were swings and slides. The bambini came in both varieties, but it was tough to tell which was which, since all of them were bundled in thick wraps that obscured every bodily feature except their eyes. Florentines live in constant fear that their kids might catch cold, so most apartments in the city are sealed airtight until summer, when the temperature outside begins to approximate that of a pizza oven.

Racing in Florence began during the Middle Ages. The earliest races were similar to those held in nearby Siena, where horses and riders representing the city's various wards competed over a treacherous course winding through cobbled streets jammed with spectators. The prize was (and is) an expensive, elaborately embroidered *palio*, or banner. In Siena, the most spent and degraded nags around were recruited to run—they went out of control so frequently that in 1262 the Sienese Council passed a resolution stating that jockeys could not be held responsible if their mounts killed or maimed any members of the crowd—but the Florentine contests were usually more gentle, featuring what one fifteenth-century writer called "the most excellent racehorses in the world." The first English thoroughbreds were probably imported into Italy in 1808 by a Neapolitan prince for use at his stud farm in Sicily, and soon thereafter thoroughbred racing was introduced in major cities all over the country. Roger Longrigg, the racing historian, says that by 1827 there was an annual meeting in Florence at a course about a mile from town. These English horses were judged so superior that they had to give thirty pounds to Tuscan horses and fourteen pounds to horses from other regions of Italy.

The first race of the day wasn't scheduled to go off until three o'clock, and that gave me time to stroll down to the rail and inspect the track. The rail was only as high as my waist. There was no mesh or chain link on top of it; if a horse happened to race very wide, you could almost reach out and touch him. Beyond the rail, two racing strips, both turf, ran parallel to each other; one of them had hurdles for jumping. The turf looked grim—tufted and beat up after a hard winter. The infield had no tote-board, no buildings, not even an ornamental pond for waterfowl. Instead, it was dotted here and there with neatly trimmed hedges that might once have been part of a steeplechase course. Past the hedges, I could see some stables, then a block of modern apartment houses, and then the Apennine Mountains. The mountains were as striking as the San Gabriels rising from the backstretch of Santa Anita, but they had to compete for attention with the wonderful dome that Filippo Brunelleschi designed during the Renaissance for Florence's great cathedral. The dome was visible off to the right, soaring into space and dominating the city's skyline.

Florentines are not a modest people. When they undertook the task of building their cathedral, they did so as much for civic pride as for religious reasons, vowing to create "the most beautiful and honorable church in Tuscany." Construction started in 1296, and the project was completed early in the fifteenth century, when Brunelleschi solved various technical problems relating to the dome's size and weight; other architects had not been able to devise a plan to support it on the drum of the cathedral. Mary McCarthy has said that Brunelleschi's dome "is the way a dome 'ought' to be done." It seems somehow to embody the Platonic ideal of domeness. Its simple, straightforward, elegant lines suggest that Brunelleschi arrived at its form only after discarding every other possible form. It has about it the spirituality of deep meditation—of a truth perceived, then rendered. It seems absolutely lacking in ego; in its purity, it abolishes the very notion of a Brunelleschi. This isn't true of Michelangelo's work, which has about it an ineradicable quality of self-aggrandizement. Michelangelo wanted to *be* God; Brunelleschi was willing to serve.

I could have stayed at the rail for quite a while, staring at the dome and letting my thoughts float into the ether, but eventually I was pulled toward the paddock by the ambulatory action of the crowd. I got my first taste of confusion when I stopped along the way to buy a program, *Galoppo e Trotto*. *Galoppo* refers to flat racing, and *Trotto* refers to harness racing. (The generic term for all types of horse racing is *ippica*.) *Galoppo e Trotto* was supposed to give me invaluable information about handicapping, but I thought it was even less useful than the semi-abstract racing papers I'd been buying in England. It told me very little about the horses entered in the day's eight races except for their weights (in kilograms), where they'd placed in their last two outings (most of them had been running at Pisa, the other major track on the Tuscan circuit), and who was riding them. Furthermore, the program was in Italian. I hadn't brought my twenty-pound Garzanti English-Italian dictionary with me, so I was certain to miss important nuances in the text. As a supplement to the program, I picked up a free tout sheet that the hippodrome had printed. It listed the favorites of the press and also the favorites of Carmine Cocca, a jockey who was going to ride in five races. Cocca had nominated just two of his mounts to win. My confusion increased. Not only was I in a foreign country, ill-informed and barely able to speak the language——the jockeys were playing with my mind.

The paddock at Cascine consists of two brick buildings roofed with the familiar red-brown tiles you see all over Tuscany. Between the buildings, there's a sort of shed where owners and trainers can have an espresso while they're waiting for the action to start. Florentines can't stand to be separated from coffee for very long, so bars are always cropping up in unlikely spots——in the basement of the central library, for instance, or at the Church of San Miniato. I stood by the paddock fence and watched the horses going round——or some of the horses. Only three of the five entrants in the first race were on parade; the two others were sequestered in numbered stalls. It didn't help to look them over, though, because the numbers bore no relation to any numbers on the program——they were too high. Apparently, trainers were under no obligation to match stall numbers with program numbers; they were putting their charges in any stall they chose. To complicate matters further, the program numbers were not the same as the horses' post positions; Doroty, the No. 1 horse, was breaking from the two hole in the starting gate, while Temezio, the No. 4 horse, was breaking from the three hole.

I had such trouble unscrambling numbers and statistics that I failed to get a bet down. That was probably fortunate, since the race was something of a mess. The horses were all two-year-olds, and they were very green. None of them had ever raced before. Pisanino, who might have had a measure of donkey blood, was so reluctant to be saddled that his trainers had to take him to a special stall that's a thoroughbred's equivalent of a padded cell. It has a door to insure privacy. For a minute or two, Pisanino could be heard kicking at the walls, but finally he emerged with a saddle on his back, looking chastened. The horses seemed uncomfortable in the starting gate, and there was some bumping around when they were released from the machinery. When they came into the home turn (the race covered just four furlongs), they went so wide that I was sure they'd wind up in the grandstand, but only poor Porto Alegre lost control. Apparently, nobody had ever taught him to change leads, so instead of wheeling into the stretch he kept running on in a straight line until he collided with a hedge. His jockey was briefly airborne. Both horse and rider came walking past the grandstand a bit later; they were scratched and bedraggled but still alive.

The second race on the card was more interesting. It gave me an opportunity to make the kind of sucker bet that invariably costs me money. Every race at Cascine has a name (Premio Ghiberti, Premio Hogarth), and this one was called the Premio Fantasio—the Fanciful Prize. Salvador Dali was entered in it. Dali was a strapping seven-year-old with a powerful frame. The groom who was walking him around the paddock had hair dyed a pumpkiny shade of orange. Over Dali's eyes, a black rectangle of cloth was draped; it covered his eye sockets and reached almost to his nose, so that he seemed ready to face a firing squad. I'd never seen anything like the cloth before; as a device to prevent skittishness, it

put blinkers to shame. I wondered if the cloth would be removed before Dali went to the post or if he'd run with it on,
transforming (as his namesake had done) the ordinary into
the surreal. In any case, Dali was an exact fit for the phe-
nomenology of the moment, and I decided to back him with
a few thousand lire.

This wasn't so easy to do. If I'd been willing to part with
ten bucks, I could have bet with one of the bookies who oc-
cupy wooden booths along the perimeter of the grandstand,
but I was thinking more in the nature of a fiver, which was
below the bookies' self-imposed limit. I had to go inside and
bet with the Florentine version of a pari-mutuel system. It
was totally non-electronic, with no flashing bulbs to indicate
odds; I had no idea what price I might be getting on Dali. I
approached a counter where twenty or thirty would-be bettors were waving notes at clerks who stood in front of several large pegboards with hooks; each hook had tissue-thin
tickets impaled on it. (The best and classiest paper in Italy is
reserved for wrapping cheese and cold cuts in delicates-
sens.) There was no queue, no semblance of order. You had
to push or be pushed forward to give birth to your transaction, just as at an Italian bank. I fumbled a little when my
turn came. It was difficult to remember a) to speak Italian,
b) to ask for Dali by program number, not post position, and
c) to count my change. Somehow, though, I got a ticket. I
didn't realize at the time how lucky I was; later in the day,
after a similar bout of push-and-shove, I was denied my
wager by a clerk who shrugged and said he was out of the
ticket I wanted.

As it happened, my faith in Salvador Dali as horse of the

moment was badly misplaced. He ran without his black veil and just barely finished the race. His tongue was hanging so far out of his mouth that I thought he might trip over it. I was about to throw my ticket away in disgust when, by chance, I noticed that I held not Dali's number but the number of Fontaineriant, the winner. Whether the error was the clerk's or my own, I don't know, but I was overjoyed to collect earnings I didn't deserve. The occurrence seemed, in true Tuscan manner, weird and beautiful all at once.

For the rest of the afternoon, I drifted around the grandstand, feeling good, with cash in my pocket and the sun on my face. I made a few more bets (or tried to), but I was really more interested in soaking up the atmosphere. Once I started to relax, my confusion gradually seeped away. Italy can be a terribly frustrating country for pilgrims raised on notions of efficiency. Nothing seems to work right, by American or British, or even French, standards; that anything works at all is considered something of a blessing. If you complain to a Florentine about the outrages you've experienced—unpredictable bus service, random mail delivery, surly waiters and clerks, cabbies who invent surcharges—he will smile ruefully and nod in agreement while simultaneously thinking what a fool you are to expect so much from life. To enjoy Italy, you've got to do a backflip into a more luxurious sense of time and learn to appreciate the simple, mundane turning about of human beings, beyond any concerns of history or politics. The people I saw in the grandstand had a marvelous presence—a physical fluidity that was precisely a result of the release from temporal pressure. They seemed less interested in the actual running of a race than in the possibility of discussing it afterward; they gathered in knots, like little families, and argued and laughed and touched each other as the world—wherever that was—went about its business.

Late in April, I went out to Cascine for the one-hundred-and-fifty-fifth running of the Corsa dell'Arno, Italy's oldest race for thoroughbreds. The race, over a mile and an eighth, is a fair test of speed and stamina. The winner earns thirty million lire, or about twenty-three thousand dollars—an enormous purse in Tuscany. This year's Arno was especially exciting, because Jorge Velasquez, billed in the local papers as *"il famoso jockey americano,"* was flying in to ride a horse called Beggar's Bridge, and to compete in a *sfida,* or challenge, against a young Irish jockey, Walter Swinburn. The jockeys were to be awarded points on the basis of how their mounts finished in the last four races on the card; the winner would receive an impressive trophy. Swinburn was not as well known as Velasquez, but he'd made a name for himself in 1981 by taking both the English Derby and the King George VI and Queen Elizabeth Stakes at Ascot aboard the ill-fated Shergar, who was later kidnapped from the Aga Khan's stables.

The weather was unpropitious on the day of the Arno. A howling wind blew through Cascine; dust off the footpaths rose in clouds, and the branches on the trees along the central boulevard rustled constantly. Hookers who were looking for early action seemed to lean against the claw-footed street lamps more for support than for advertisement. But a big crowd had turned out for the race anyway—maybe five thousand people, among them more hard-core racing fans than I'd ever seen at Cascine before. Guys who looked like Dean Martin and Al Martino were smoking slow cigarettes and giving the eye to anything in skirts. There were toupees in evidence, and also neck chains, exploded noses, stubby cigars, and hives of teased blond hair. I couldn't figure out where all these high rollers had come from. Ordinarily, Florentines are rather elegant and conservative, dressed in somber colors that reflect the monochromatic stones of the city, but these characters were done up in Vegas neon.

The crowd continued to grow, and I had to wait for a few minutes before I got a stool at the horseshoe-shaped counter of the *tavola calda,* or hot table, that serves as the hippodrome's restaurant. The tavola calda is a delight, compared with American racetrack cuisine. There is no menu. A harried waitress tells you what kinds of pasta are available as a first course, and you make your selection and help yourself to the bottles of wine and mineral water on the counter. For entertainment, you read *Galoppo e Trotto* or watch the open kitchen, where cooks in T-shirts and abused aprons labor in a matrix of grease and steam. The cooks shout at each other; they throw their hands into the air. After the pasta, the waitress usually offers you roast veal or pork, or maybe *bistecca alla fiorentina*—a thick steak grilled over a wood fire, then dabbed with olive oil and salt. The third course is fruit and pecorino, although if you are brave you can have a pastry instead. The tab for the meal at the tavola calda comes to seven or eight dollars. The only drawback is that the meal gives you a false feeling of security; losing bets don't seem so awful on a full stomach.

I walked up to the top level of the grandstand to watch the first race from a glassed-in area behind the last row of seats. I had to peer over the shoulders of some miltant grandmas who'd borrowed folding chairs from somewhere and arranged them in a phalanx in front of the windows. The race turned into a horror show when Uncle Table broke down in the stretch. His rider, Signorina Villa, took a spill. Meanwhile, Uncle Table got up on his three good legs and tried to hobble home. He had that frustrated, panicky look you often notice in horses right after they've broken down; it makes you think they have no cushioning image of catastrophe in their brains, nothing to soften the blow. After a while, two grooms stopped him. They grabbed his reins and led him across the infield, moving aside temporary fences so that he could get back to the stable by the most direct route. The horse was in such pain that he couldn't make much progress. He'd hobble for a few steps; then he'd quit and toss his head around. Finally, some other men, who seemed to have positions of authority, intercepted the grooms. The men held a lengthy consultation while Uncle Table hobbled and tossed his head. Nobody gave him a shot to kill the pain. He just kept hobbling while the men talked. One of them signaled for a worker across the infield to bring over a tractor that had a green cart behind it, but the cart was much too rickety to support Uncle Table's weight. Next, somebody called for a VW van, but it was clear even from the stands that no horse would fit inside. The dumbness of it all would have been comic if Uncle Table hadn't been hurting so badly. Almost a half hour passed before a horse van requisitioned from a distant parking lot arrived. Uncle Table was shoved up its gangplank and driven away, headed, perhaps, for the Tuscan version of the glue factory.

The *sfida* was not supposed to begin until the fifth race, but Velasquez had a mount, Foden Warrior, in the fourth, and I went down to watch him in the paddock. The press crew was watching him, too, with cameras at the ready. He came blinking out of the jockeys' room into the sun, looking a little puzzled and ill at ease, as though he'd gone to sleep in a familiar bed and awakened in a land where everything was the same but different. He fiddled with the waistband of his breeches and stared solemnly into the middle distance. Velasquez is usually pretty cocky before a race, but I guess Italy had shaken him up some. I thought he had a slight case of nerves. The shirt he wore had a big star on the chest, and I'm sure he was anxious about living up to it. The pressure was on him to perform. The hippodrome was strictly a bush-league track for him, and he really had nothing to gain by riding there, no matter how much money he might be paid for his appearance—he was already a wealthy man. If he rode well, he would only confirm what everybody had known in advance—that he was a world-class jockey. But if he had a sorry afternoon he would tarnish his reputation; for decades afterward Florentines would talk about how Tuscan riders had outshone *il famoso americano*. So I respected Velasquez for taking a risk that most jockeys of his caliber would have been happy to avoid.

Once Velasquez was in the saddle, he seemed much less nervous. The kind of calm that sailors get when they step on board ship crept over him. The horse was his fulcrum; it lent him a sense of stability in the midst of surrounding strangeness. He reached down and patted Foden Warrior on the neck, and then he took the reins in hand. When he glided by the photographers, his face broke into an unexpectedly brilliant smile. It was a smile he'd mastered in countless paddocks and winner's circles over the years, but it still had a touch of unalloyed pleasure in it, because Velasquez was up there on horseback, alive in every cell of his body, while the rest of us had our feet planted on the ground.

Foden Warrior was a nice little horse, quite well behaved, with a healthy sheen to his coat, but he was only the third favorite in the betting. The crowd was going to make Velasquez prove his skill before they'd give him any edge. I didn't think Velasquez' agent would have let him travel to Europe unless he'd got some assurance that Jorge's mounts would be primed to win, so I put my lire on Foden Warrior. Velasquez gave the horse a perfect ride, urging him to join the leaders at the head of the stretch, and then turning him loose on the long run-in. Foden Warrior had plenty to spare and won much more easily that his form would have indicated.

Before the fifth race, Walter Swinburn joined Velasquez in the paddock. He is twenty-one, but he could pass for sixteen; his altar-boy potential is still intact. He has pale, unscarred skin, and he projects the humility of spirit that all successful young jockeys seem to share. It's the losers who snarl and get rank. Swinburn's father, Wally, is also a jockey, and he happened to be in Italy, too—down in Rome, where he was riding in a big stakes race. The trip was on the order of a family holiday for the Swinburns, but I had a feeling that Velasquez was going to spoil Walter's part of it. The victory on Foden Warrior had pumped him up, and now he was strutting around the paddock with a strong proprietary air. He chatted with grooms and trainers, and when he got on Sandaletto, his mount for the race, he looked so confident that he sent people dashing for the pari-mutuel windows. He booted Sandaletto home without much bother, although Starscki ("Starsky and Hutch" is a popular series on Italian TV) made a run at him near the wire. Swinburn, on Lord Quinto Romano, finished third.

Velasquez' hot hand didn't last through the Corsa dell'Arno, though. The horse he'd been assigned to ride, Beggar's Bridge, was rumored to be a course specialist, who'd won often at Cascine in the past, but I'd seen him race once and he'd looked sick. Choco Air, a handsome bay colt out of a Never Bend mare, had whipped him soundly. Beggar's Bridge had dragged past the stands in a heavy lather; he'd seemed out of shape, in need of serious conditioning. At seven, he was the oldest horse entered in the Arno (Choco Air was entered in it, too), and he was conceding over twenty pounds to some of his younger rivals. In the paddock, he shambled around, as though a premonition of defeat had infected him; he had no perkiness, no brightness. Swinburn's mount, Baldog, looked much better, but Baldog had been out only once all year, and he probably wasn't fit enough yet to pose a threat.

Weight was an important factor in the Arno. The winner, Il Taischan, carried only one hundred pounds, compared with a hundred and twenty-four for Beggar's Bridge and a hundred and thirty-one for Choco Air. He was kept in reserve until the stretch, while other horses, including Choco Air, made the pace. Immediately after the final turn, he ac-

celerated. Several others—Efidanville, Mistan, My Sea—
joined him, but he was able to pull away and cross the wire
first, much to the disappointment of the crowd, who'd let
him go off at fairly generous odds. Il Taischan was bred at
Ballinagall Stud, in Ireland; he is a solid, long-striding horse
with talent to bank against the future. As for Beggar's
Bridge, he waddled in eighth with the sweat pouring off him,
a prime candidate for a vacation.

Velasquez didn't win either of the last two races, but the
sfida trophy was his anyway, because Swinburn's mounts
were such stiffs. The only horse Swinburn had who really
figured—Riden, in the seventh—finished a miserable
fourth. No doubt Swinburn was happy to strip off his Italian
silks, climb back into his street clothes, and head for Great
Britain, where he would soon be riding a filly called Circus
Ring, in the illustrious Coronation Stakes at Ascot. For Velasquez, the trip to Cascine had been more rewarding. In
five races, he'd had two firsts and a second, so he could wing
home to the States with his reputation enhanced, knowing
that he'd lent a bit of international luster to the Arno and
made some new friends in the bargain.

The last time I went to Cascine, in mid-May, the hippodrome was already showing the effects of the oppressive
heat that begins to grip the city toward the end of every
spring. The track had always been a lazy sort of place, con-
ducive to meditative driftiness, but now an outright torpor
had set in. The grass on the racing strip hadn't been mowed
for weeks. It was at least six inches long, brown in patches,
and sprouting weeds. Only four horses could be recruited to

run in the first race, and they were pretty tired. Two of them—Babusch and my old pal Fontaineriant—had been rested for just three days, while another, Assio, had been rested for just two. The four horses in the second race had all run against each other eleven days earlier. Apparently, there was a critical shortage of thoroughbreds in Tuscany. Throughout the afternoon, I saw so many familiar faces at the paddock that I felt bad for not bringing along any carrots or lumps of sugar to offer up on my palm.

In spite of the mediocre racing, I enjoyed myself, because Cascine was one of the few spots where I could be sure to escape the tourists. They had been descending on the city in a steady stream since Easter, filling the hotels and *pensioni,* and traveling everywhere in packs, like the walking dead. When they went to a museum, they did so in groups of twenty or thirty, trailing vacantly behind guides who had terrific repertoires of platitudes. The museums made no move to control the groups, so it was virtually impossible to visit the Uffizi or the Pitti Palace without having to stand on tiptoe to catch a glimpse of the paintings. In addition, the guards at the Uffizi were always going out on lightning strikes, often for two or three days straight; the museum was closed so often that a small band of irate tourists actually staged a demonstration to protest. The splendor of the Renaissance was slowly disappearing beneath an ooze of boosterism and failed bureaucracy.

In some ways, the great soul of Florence was easier to touch at the hippodrome than it was at more highly touted places. Nobody tried to sell you cameos or overpriced leather goods or distorted little statues of David. The prosciutto sandwiches came on real Tuscan bread, and the chianti was rough, with a peasant edge to it. If you were willing to spend a while down at the rail, staring at the city, you learned to experience Brunelleschi's dome the way Florentines have been experiencing it for centuries—not merely as a work of art but as a constant presence in your life, reminding you of what human beings, in their better moments, can accomplish.

THREE

CALIFORNIA AGAIN

Whether we live by the seaside,
or by the lakes and rivers, or
on the prairie, it concerns us
to attend to the nature of fishes,
since they are not phenomena
confined to certain localities only,
but forms and phases of the life
in nature universally dispersed.
—H. D. Thoreau, *A Week on the*
Concord and Merrimack Rivers

※ ※

Hat Creek
and the McCloud

Every autumn, I try to make a trip into the mountains of northern California to do some trout-fishing, and this past year was no exception. I was more eager than ever, in fact, because I hadn't done any fishing for a while, and I felt an acute biological need for open spaces. On our return from Europe, we'd settled in San Francisco, and the honk and nonsense of the city was already getting to me. I suppose the noise wasn't really any worse than the noise of London or Florence, but it had an echo of permanence about it. Gone were the days of carefree wandering. Anyway, I got out of bed one morning and stared through my apartment window at the tree on my block and noticed that six or seven of its pauperish leaves had turned red. That was my signal—a mere urban reflection of what would be going on in the Trinity Alps or the Cascade Range.

In my closet, I had a shoebox file of fishing maps, and I pulled it out to help me decide which river to fish. I chose Hat Creek, a famous California stream in Siskiyou County I'd never hit before. Hat Creek flows south through the granite and lava of the Cascades until it dead-ends in Lassen Volcanic National Park. In its lower reaches, it is among the richest trout streams in the United States, on a par with the Firehole River, in Wyoming, and the Letort Spring Run, in Pennsylvania. It is capable of producing enough food to support as many as three thousand two hundred trout over five miles of water. All the trout in lower Hat Creek are wild, not hatchery-reared, and they can grow to considerable size. This section of the stream is elegant and challenging. It attracts anglers from all over the world. Fishing pressure is often intense, especially during the legendary insect hatches that explode in clockwork fashion in the summer months— little yellow stone flies in June, pale morning duns in July, tricorythodes spinners in August. In order to preserve the quality of lower Hat Creek, the California Department of Fish and Game has instituted a stringent set of regulations. Only artificial flies and lures with single barbless hooks may be used, so that fish can be released with as little damage to them as possible. (A study done at Hat Creek in 1973 revealed that anglers let go sixty-three per cent of the fish they'd hooked.) The daily creel limit is two trout. The trout must be at least eighteen inches long—big fish, that is, the kind that set your heart to pumping.

Hat Creek is so productive because it's a spring creek, pure and translucent, fed primarily by underground springs rather than rain or snowmelt. Like most spring creeks, it has a high concentration of bound carbon dioxide—sixty to eighty parts per million, as compared to ten or twenty for an average stream. As the creek percolates up through the volcanic subsoil of the region, the carbon dioxide in it dissolves deposits of marl and lime that have formed around the fossilized skeletons of crustaceans, snails, shellfish, and plants.

This makes the creek very alkaline. It has large quantities of calcium and magnesium carbonates. Alkalinity encourages an abundance of insect life—particularly of those species most favored by trout. It also promotes weed growth (weeds provide cover for fish and oxygenate a stream through photosynthesis) and, in general, helps to create excellent habitat for German browns and rainbows. The trout of Hat Creek are stocky, brilliantly colored, and difficult to catch even in autumn, after the tourists have all gone home.

I spent the evening before I left sorting through my tackle. I wanted to get rid of the worthless stuff, but I couldn't bring myself to throw out anything. Nostalgia seems to infuse every aspect of fishing, including the gear. When I came across a handful of streamer flies tied for steelhead, I started thinking about my friend Paul Deeds, who taught me almost everything I know about those ungovernable fish. I hadn't seen Deeds for more than a year. I'd sent him some postcards, but I knew even as I mailed them that they were destined to wind up in the flyblown cellar of his house. Deeds never answers his mail. He doesn't have much affection for the telephone, either—he regards it as an instrument of torture. I'd called him a couple of times since I'd been back, just to say hello, but I'd felt as though I were talking to a doorjamb. What we'd shared could not in any way be counted as conversations. I thought I'd give him one more try, though, because I missed him and I was in the mood for company on Hat Creek.

I dialed Deeds's number. The phone rang and rang. I could see him sitting in his ratty kitchen with a cup of coffee at his elbow, looking out into the prune orchard that surrounds his place and hoping that the ringing would stop.

"Who is it?" he asked when he picked up the receiver. He must have been holding it yards from his mouth; I could barely hear him.

I told him who it was, and what I had in mind.

"You're crazy," Deeds said. "Hat Creek is too crowded. There'll be all kinds of people around."

"It's almost October, Paul. It won't be too bad."

"Maybe not for a city person," he said.

Deeds can be very stubborn when it comes to matters of principle or opinion. From his reluctance to discuss Hat Creek, I figured that he'd probably been there once when four or five other anglers were on the river, and that this horrible *crowd* had so disconcerted him that he swore never to return.

"If you were making a trip, where would you go?" I asked.

"McCloud River," he said. "Down in the canyon, near the Nature Conservancy preserve. I'd camp at Ah-Di-Na Meadow. I'd fish downstream from there to Ladybug Creek. Hang on for a second, my dog wants to get out."

The only part of the McCloud that I was familiar with was a tame stretch than runs parallel to Interstate 5 near Dunsmuir. It's a decent but unspectacular stream in that region, similar to many other streams that border highways and are subject to the passing fancies of motorist-anglers. The McCloud that runs through the canyon is completely different—far less accessible and so less popular. It flows through rugged terrain that still has a few bears and mountain lions. In the canyon, the trout are wild.

"It's getting cold out there," Deeds said, when he came back on the line.

"You don't think it'll be crowded on the McCloud?"

"I sincerely doubt it. The road in is about eight miles of bad dirt."

I checked a map of Siskiyou County. The town of McCloud was just fifty miles or so from where I'd be. "Suppose I fish Hat Creek first, then meet you in McCloud?"

"I can't just drop everything and take off."

This made me laugh. Deeds is divorced. He has no job. He lives off his faltering prune crop and the small portfolio of stocks and bonds that he inherited.

"What can be so pressing?" I asked. "The harvest is over."

"There's still the dog to be fed."

After further negotiations, he agreed to call me in the morning. I told him not to be too late, since I wanted to get an early start, but I didn't have to worry. Deeds woke me just after six o'clock, while the sky was still black.

"Friday at the McCloud Hotel," he said. "I'll meet you there about noon."

Almost nothing makes me happier than to leave on a fishing trip. I feel like I'm doing something active for a change instead of hanging around on a street corner waiting for a bus to jump the curb and run me over. One of the secret terrors of the age is that we are all dying slowly of complacency. I carried my tackle to the car and put it in the trunk. The sky was red now, streaked with pink clouds. I could tell from the haze and stillness that it was going to be hot. By the time I'd reached Redding, around midmorning, the temperature had risen to eighty-four degrees. Redding is at the northern tip of the Sacramento Valley. It's a wonderful spot to experience heat, since it's hemmed in by two mountain ranges—the Salmons and the Cascades—and the air in town moves not at all.

I stopped at a tackle shop that specializes in materials and gear for those who fish with flies. The clerk told me that the fishing on Hat Creek had only been fair for the last week or so. He said that I shouldn't look for much in the way of insect hatches, except for orange caddis flies and maybe a few blue-wing olives. The trout would most likely be feeding below the surface. They'd go for nymphs and streamers. (Nymphs imitate insect larvae; streamers imitate baitfish.) He suggested that I use a fly line with a sinking tip. I bought one and also some stone-fly nymphs and some leeches. When I asked the clerk about places to stay, he recommended Lava Creek Lodge, in Glenburn.

That afternoon, I got my first glimpse of Hat Creek. It snuck up on me without any fanfare. I went over a highway bridge just past Burney and saw a stream on both sides of me and then a sign that said HAT CREEK. I turned the car around and pulled down an access road that led to a picnic area by the water. After Deeds's warning, I expected the picnic tables to be occupied by hundreds of chubby guys in T-shirts and funny hats, but nobody was there. Nobody was fishing, either. I walked to the creek and knelt on the bank. The water was very clear. I could see almost to the streambed—about five feet down, I guessed. There were weeds—red, brown, purple, many shades of green—shifting around in the current. The motion had a witchery to it. In spite of what the clerk had told me, there was a good hatch of mayflies going on. The bugs floated toward heaven on lacy wings.

The setting was so serene, and so perfect for trout, that it was hard to remember that Hat Creek was once a decimated stream. Its transformation began in 1968, around the time that the Department of Fish and Game came under pressure from conservation-minded angling organizations for having let the quality of trout-fishing in California deteriorate. The department had been slow to protect prime habitat against environmental degradation, and there were fewer and fewer productive wild trout streams around. To make up for its losses, the department relied on what's known as a "put-and-take" program. In essence, the state kept dumping millions of small, hatchery-reared trout into rivers as fast as anglers reeled in the old ones. That's pretty fast—hatchery fish are easy to catch. At the hatchery, they've been trained to answer the dinner bell. They'll chase after almost any type of bait—worms, salmon eggs, even mini-marshmallows. They've never learned any survival skills, so when they're planted in a stream, they panic and school together in fear. Most of them are hooked right away. Predators pitch in to make short work of others. Only a few hatchery fish in any river manage to last from one season to the next.

The put-and-take program was (and is) popular with weekend anglers who were only interested in filling their creel, but it didn't satisfy the purists. The project to reclaim lower Hat Creek was an attempt to please them. When the project started, trash fish made up about ninety-five per cent

of the creek's population. They'd eaten or otherwise inter-
fered with most of the native trout in the project area—a
three-and-a-half-mile stretch between Lake Britton and
Baum Lake. Biologists went to the stream and captured wild
strains of rainbow and German brown for later restocking.
The stream was then treated with chemicals. About seven
tons of trash fish eventually turned belly-up—Sacramento
suckers, hardmouths, buffalo fish. Next, a barrier was constructed at the northern end of the creek to prevent the
trash fish in Lake Britton from moving upstream. The wild
trout were planted again, and they flourished. They had
more food, less danger and competition. The project was
such a success that, in 1971, the department established a
more elaborate wild trout program to restore and perpetuate quality angling throughout the state. Currently, seven-
teen streams and a lake are designated for wild trout
management.

For a while, I sat on the riverbank, watching the insects
hatch. The sunshine felt good, a tonic to the bones. Every
now and then, I saw a dimple on the water when a trout rose
to swallow a fallen bug. I had to stifle my desire to run to the
car and grab my rod. The sitting still was an act of disci-
pline. The notion was to be calm instead of frenzied, as I
usually am on the first day. I concentrated on the creek, its
flow, the channels where fish were feeding, trying to commit
the details to memory. It takes a long time before you begin
to see things with any degree of actuality. After thirty minutes of meditation, I got to my feet, stretched my legs, and
drove to the lodge.

. . . .

Glenburn is not so much a real town as a name on a map. It's located in the Fall River Valley, at an elevation of about thirty-five hundred feet. The valley has a cowboy feel to it. Beef cattle are the major agricultural industry, so pasture-land is conspicuous. I passed fields of grass and alfalfa, of grain hay. There were sprinklers in the fields—the sort with long pipes and spoked wheels. Blackbirds were riding them. I saw hundreds of mallards overhead, beginning their annual migration, winging south along the course of the Fall River. Like Hat Creek, the Fall is spring-fed and extremely productive. It supports an estimated two thousand trout to the mile. The property that borders the river is all privately owned. The only way to fish the Fall (unless you've got a rancher friend) is by boat. A boat opens up twelve miles of countryside. You drift by farms and ranches, weathered barns, aspens, grazing cattle. Sometimes you catch a glimpse of Mt. Shasta with its eternally snowcapped peak.

Lava Creek is a relatively new place. It consists of a lodge with a bar and a restaurant. The lodge sits right on the edge of a pretty little lake called Eastman. There are a few cabins, too, set among scrubby pines, and I rented one. It came equipped with a dented pot-and-pan combo and several back issues of *Family Circle* and *Cosmopolitan*. I don't think I've ever rented a cabin anywhere that didn't have at least two or three women's magazines on the kitchen table. Some Gideon-like organization must be responsible for distributing them to resorts throughout the Pacific Northwest.

After I unloaded the car, I took a stroll to see if I could ferret out any hot angling tips from the locals. Near my cabin, I ran into a young guy in a down vest who was chopping wood. By the look of the pile he'd stacked against a shed, he was preparing for a cold winter. His name was Kyle. He and his wife managed the place. He told me that Hat Creek was going to be a tough mother to fish. I'd have to cast perfectly if I hoped to score, because the water was clear and slow-moving and wouldn't disguise my mistakes. Most of the big trout had already been caught, then released, and they were especially wary. Kyle knew guides who refused to let their clients even *try* to cast. Instead, the clients had to *deposit* their flies on the water, then strip line from their reels by hand until the flies floated in front of feeding trout. For novices, Kyle said, the best spot on the creek was fifty yards of broken, riffly water that flowed out from a Pacific Gas and Electric Company powerhouse. The riffles helped to hide a faulty presentation. Your fly didn't have to land as smoothly there, since the water was in a state of perturbation and even real insects bobbed around like mad. "You try there first," Kyle said.

I got to the powerhouse at six o'clock. It was just off the main highway, down a well-maintained utility company road. Four men were already fishing in the riffles. They'd left enough space for me to sneak in among them, but I hated it when somebody did that to me, so I put on my waders, climbed over a stile, and walked upstream toward slacker water that rolled idly through a meadow. Some black Angus cattle were plodding around on the opposite hillside, their heads lowered to the ground. The trees at the edge of the meadow were incense cedars. Their bark was red-brown, ridged and covered with scales.

The calm attitude I'd cultivated during my meditation vanished completely once I had my rod assembled. Trout were rising everywhere, making circles with their lips on the smooth, slick creek. Occasionally, I heard an explosion—some really monstrous lunker leaping into the air to nab a bug. I couldn't decide what the fish were taking, so I tried a leech that I'd bought in Redding. Properly speaking, leeches are ugly, segmented, bloodsucking worms of the type that attached themselves to Humphrey Bogart in *The African Queen*. The imitation is not so repulsive. It's a feathery black fly that's best fished just under the surface.

Once I had the leech tied to my leader, I moved closer to the stream. I wanted to wade it, like the men below me in the riffles, but it was too deep where I was, and I had to do my casting from shore. Whenever you're casting, the idea is to fall into a hypnotic rhythm, so that you and the rod become one—so that *thinking* becomes impossible—but I failed to accomplish that. The rod and I were bitter enemies. It wouldn't do a thing I asked it to. I kept hooking the leech on the tall star nettles and giant mulleins behind me. It seemed to me that if I went further upstream, where the banks were not so overgrown, I might do better, but the soil there proved to be marshy and I slid into it up to my knees.

The whole scenario would have been tragic if it hadn't happened to me so many times before. One of the few advantages of maturity is that petty failures no longer make you break rods, get drunk, and curse at strangers. I brushed the muck from my waders, then wiped my hands on my shirt. (In a pinch, fishing clothes are a tolerable substitute for towels or handkerchiefs.) I snipped off the leech and tied on an orange caddis. It was a dry fly, so it floated. With its wings propped up, it looked like a princely specimen, but it found no takers. Neither did the mosquito I tried next.

As I was trading the mosquito for a black ant, I glanced up and saw a mangy cocker spaniel running toward me. For some reason, fishermen's dogs are always friendly. They love to dance around and do tricks and stick out their tongues in a totally joyous way. Some of their masters' joy at being outside in the good world God made must get trans-mitted to them. I patted the spaniel on the head, and he licked my hand. His master came along in a minute or two—a stocky guy who was grunting from the effort of walking. He'd chewed his cigar to an interesting mass. I asked him how he'd done, and he said he'd taken two minor-league trout the night before, but that he'd been skunked this eve-ning. "The moon, it's almost full," he said. "Those fish have been stuffing themselves on caddis all month long."

At dusk, I packed it in. About seven or eight men were in the riffles now, pressed in much too tightly. I watched them for a bit—they were all using nymphs and streamers—but none of them got any action. I opened a can of beer and drove to the lodge. The country night was sweet. I pushed the accelerator to the floor, enjoying a rush of speed, and the liberating sensation of being unpoliced. Traffic cops are scarce in the Fall River Valley. The dark, twisty roads im-pose the laws. I pushed the radio button and on came Char-ley Pride singing "You're So Good When You're Bad." A little later, the white clapboard face of Glenburn church jumped out at me. It was built in 1886. Services are still held in it once a month, even in winter, when the deacons have to fire up a potbellied stove to ward off the chill.

. . .

There was frost on my windshield when I left the lodge the next morning. I was tempted to go back inside, crawl under the covers, and read *Family Circle* until the sun was higher in the sky, but I pushed myself forward, into the wintry air and then out into the valley. A man and his son were launching a skiff in the Fall, and they both waved and smiled, blowing clouds of breath. The leaves of the aspens along the river had died some more during the night, and they were a brighter yellow than ever. A powder of new snow was on the mountains. The light was intense, a shock to the eyes.

I hoped that I'd be rewarded for bucking the cold, but the powerhouse riffles were again occupied by several anglers. One guy was wearing earmuffs and gloves. The sight of this coward so unnerved me that I had a very Deedsian reaction and took off in a huff for the picnic area I'd stopped at the first afternoon. It was still deserted. I followed a trail that went under the highway bridge into another meadow, thinking it might lead me to a secret, uninhabited, fruitful run of water.

The trail took me around a bend in the creek. Ahead, I saw a short stretch of fast water. It wasn't as fast as the riffle water, but it was fast enough to sink a wet fly. I chose a stone-fly nymph from my fly box. Western stone flies emerge in spring and summer, but, as nymphs, they're present in streams at other times, and they're an important food for trout. The fly must be fished deep to be effective, so I wrapped a little piece of lead around my line. This made casting more awkward. I kept wishing for an insect hatch; the trout would start feeding, and I'd know which imitation to use. But the bugs stayed quiet all morning, and I had to fish blind. Around one o'clock, hunger got the best of me, and I walked to the car to eat. I had a sandwich of Safeway cheese, and then an apple, and then I had a nap. I must have been tired, because I didn't wake until midafternoon. I went to the creek and washed my face, then drove to the power-house again. All the back-and-forth driving was beginning to take the shine off my fishing experience.

On the utility company road, I had to brake to a halt when a porcupine raced in front of me. Actually, "raced" is too strong a word to apply to any porcupine, even if the animal is moving at top speed. The porcupine waddled. It seemed as surprised to see me as I was to see it. In the mountains, you get used to the chipmunk and squirrel kamikazes who are always darting in front of your tires, risking their exis-tence for a thrill, but porcupines are pretty rare. They ap-pear to have stumbled into the wrong century, and they're not happy about it. Once this porcupine made it across the road, he waddled into a gully and started climbing a hum-mock, toward the shelter of some toyon bushes. The hum-mock was wet from the morning's frost, and the porcupine had difficulty with his footing. He'd almost make it to the toyons and then the earth would give beneath his feet and down he'd roll, quills-first, into the gully. The show was so good that I switched off the motor and sat there watching him. The curious thing was that he never bothered to look back. I knew that if I were doing the climbing, and I sensed the presence of an intruder, I'd be peeking over my shoul-der whenever I could. Maybe that's a good definition of neu-rosis——to be constantly peeking over your shoulder to check what might be wrong. The porcupine was incredibly determined. He must have fallen fifteen times before he finally reached his goal. I wanted to applaud him. In fact, I would have applauded him if I thought he'd care, but he didn't even stop at the top of the hummock to celebrate. He wasn't anywhere close to being human.

For once, nobody was in the powerhouse riffles—I had the spot to myself. I tied on a new leader with a very fine taper and, to that, I tied a caddis nymph. I waded into the creek rather cautiously—the current was strong—and began to cast. It went well for a change. I was able to concentrate on what I was doing, but after thirty fishless minutes, a thought unrelated to angling came into my head, and then another thought came—inconsequential, both these thoughts—and I drifted off in pursuit of them. Of course, I had an immediate strike. A trout with a sense of humor grabbed the nymph while I was playing around with the little fist in my skull. The bite was like a reminder from nature. It brought me back to attention, but then I drifted off again, into a fantasy about how I'd tell Kyle of Lava Creek that I'd hooked and lost a terrific fish. The fantasy gave way to speculation about why anglers are pathological liars, and before I knew it I'd worked myself to the end of the riffles.

I took a rest on the bank. Late-afternoon sunshine was coming through the cedar branches. Suddenly, insects began to hatch. It was very exciting, because I could see them so clearly—orange caddis flies. I snapped a spool with a floating line into my reel and tied on an imitation caddis, size 18. There was some water that was already in shade, and I worked it first. I made short, delicate casts to cut down on mistakes. I knew that I was doing a good job of presenting the fly, but I was still surprised when a rainbow trout took it. I had so little line on the water that I landed the trout with no trouble. It was about thirteen inches long, stout and boxy, bearing the bright pinks and reds and silvers of a wild trout. Hatchery fish have the same colors, but they always seem muted, like bad reproductions of great art. When I gripped the trout to remove my hook, I could feel its flailing muscles, a tremendous focusing of power. Because the hook was barbless, it slipped out easily, leaving just a tiny tear in the trout's lip. I released it into the creek and watched it dart into the depths. Nothing disappears as quickly as a trout redeemed.

That evening, after dinner, I went to the lodge for a drink. No doubt I was looking for a chance to mention my trout, but I couldn't get a word in edgewise with the four other angler-guests at the bar. They were fly-fishing bullies—the kind of guys who dress in unsoiled flannel, down, and khaki garments and spend thousands of dollars on tackle and far-flung vacations. These bullies are always yakking about their last trip to New Zealand or Patagonia, and it's very depressing to listen to them, since by their insistence on the value of all the things in life that *don't* matter, they violate the essence of the sport—which combines, as Izaak Walton noted, humility and a calmness of spirit. I only lasted through a single bourbon. Instead of going to my cabin, I walked to Eastman Lake and sat on the shore for a few minutes, just staring at the moonlight on the water. Moonlight never gets old.

. . .

The next morning, I left for the McCloud, using Mt. Shasta as my marker. "Shasta is a fire-mountain," wrote the naturalist, John Muir, "an old volcano gradually accumulated and built up into the deep blue of the sky by successive eruptions of molten lava." It dominates the southern Cascades—a dissected tableland of basaltic sheets, mudflows, and ash, capped by volcanic cones. The cone of Shasta is over fourteen thousand feet high. Its crater is still hot. Live glaciers still scour its sides (most of them are on the north slope), and they feed hundreds of streams, including the McCloud. The aboriginal residents of the region were Shastans, members of the Hokan family, who gathered acorns and manzanita berries, and killed salmon, bear, and deer. Another tribe—the Modocs—were the Shastans' enemies. They were immortalized in a best-selling book that also lifted the mountain into the realm of popular myth—Joaquin Miller's *Life Among the Modocs*, written in 1873. Miller was a bearded, boisterous man, a precursor of the modern author/self-publicist. He wore outrageous cowboy clothes even in polite society—they loved him in London, where he showed up in chaps to take tea—and he did his damndest to wring poetry from monumental stone. The poetry could be pretty unrelenting at times:

> Lonely as God, and white as a winter
> moon, Mount Shasta starts up sudden
> and solitary from the black forests of
> Northern California . . .

Another poet who found inspiration in the country around Shasta was William Randolph Hearst. Hearst is not generally included in literary company, but—according to W. A. Swanberg, his biographer—he "always enjoyed scribbling verses." Hearst had a five-story medieval manor house on 67,000 inland acres of virgin forest near the McCloud. The house was known as Wyntoon, except to Hearst's mistress, Marion Davies, who hated the place and called it Spittoon. Ms. Davies spent most of her time there playing backgammon. During the Second World War, when Hearst developed a fear that the Japanese might shell San Simeon from boats on the Pacific, he moved to Wyntoon for two years. One of his poems—he had the nerve to print it in the New York *Journal-American*—was composed while he was in exile. It's about the mystery of life, and it has even more overwrought metaphors per poetic square inch than Miller's work.

The name "McCloud" is a corruption of McLeod—Alexander McLeod, a trader for the Hudson's Bay Company, who discovered the river, in 1829. It was a grand stream then. It had large annual runs of seagoing fish, like salmon and steelhead. The fish traveled inland from the ocean for almost two hundred miles to spawn. The rainbow trout now in the river are probaby descendants of anadromous specimens who became landlocked through volcanic and seismic changes and lost their migratory urge. An egg-taking station was established on the river, in 1872, so that McCloud strains of salmon and rainbow trout could be distributed worldwide. The heyday of angling on the McCloud was in the early 1900s, when fishing clubs owned most of the stream. In the 1940s, Shasta Dam was built. It put an end to the anadromous runs and significantly altered the quality of trout-fishing.

The soil along the McCloud is very rocky, much too thin to be farmed. Ranching has been a mainstay here since the 1850s, and so has lumbering. Almost all of the open conifer forest that grows on the mountain slopes has been logged over. (Hearst's acreage was one of the last accessible virgin parcels to go.) The forest has Douglas firs, white firs, sugar pines, yellow pines, and ponderosa pines. The towns I passed through were all logging towns. McCloud had been a logging town, too. The McCloud Lumber Company incorporated it, in 1896, but they'd vanished from the scene, and now an investment company owned it. Apparently, the investment company was turning it into a retirement community——at least that's what I gathered when I drove down the main street. There were septuagenarians everywhere. McCloud was absolutely jammed with them. They were buying papers and medications at the pharmacy, taking constitutionals in the clean mountain air, and keeping an eye out for the encroachment of crime in any of its multifarious forms. Quite a number of them were sitting in chairs and rockers on the porch of the McCloud Hotel——so many, in fact, that I had to drive around the block twice before I recognized Paul Deeds among them.

Deeds has an ability to blend in with almost any group. The only time I ever saw him stand out was some years ago when I invited him to join me for dinner at a fancy restaurant. He came with his hair slicked down and his beard trimmed, and he was so uneasy throughout the evening that I knew I'd made an error in judgment. "Why in the hell do the put ice cubes on the carrots and celery?" he asked when our waiter brought a relish tray. He plucked the cubes off the veggies and surreptitiously dumped them under the table. During the evening, he perceived several other offenses against decency and freely commented on them. When the check arrived on a sterling platter, he seized it and laughed so loudly that the couple at the next table shot us killer glances. "This would have bought me ten meals at the Tip-Top Café," Deeds said, weeping from the humor of it all. Such occasions make me wonder if Deeds and I would even be friends if it weren't for fishing.

Deeds was in his element on the hotel porch. A baseball cap on his head, he rocked in his rocker and paused every now and then to scratch himself. He looked to be half asleep, caught up in some rural fantasia, but this turned out to be a guise. He was actually mad at me for being late. I explained to him that my progress had been affected by the cows who kept wandering across the highway, and by the logging trucks that kept barreling around blind curves— often with fourteen of their eighteen wheels aloft.

"We're going to have a hard time getting set up before dark," Deeds said. "I just want to be straight about who's responsible."

We had another argument when I rebelled against the contents of Deeds's cooler. All he had in there were eggs, bacon, potatoes, bread, coffee, a six-pack of Diet Dr Pepper, and about eight pounds of ground chuck. The absence of anything remotely green or leafy was appalling, and I insisted that he let me pick up some salad stuff at the market.

"What are you afraid of?" Deeds asked. "Scurvy?"

I wouldn't answer him. He put his truck in gear, and we started out of town.

The bad dirt hit us after we'd climbed a saddle of land, then dropped down to McCloud Reservoir. Pavement gave way to pocked and rutted ground that bore the deeply carved scars of flooding. Deeds had to proceed at a crawl so we wouldn't snap our spines. It took us a while to reach the crest of the road. From there, we had a fine view of Shasta. We began our descent into the canyon. Black oaks and big-leaf maples were mixed in among the pines. We passed through some stands of virgin timber. There were Douglas firs three hundred feet tall. A pair of red-shafted flickers flew by, flashing their salmon-colored wings. Farther on, we spooked a black-tailed doe and her two fawns. They'd been browsing near some manzanita bushes. Unlike my porcupine pal, the deer stopped to look back once they'd put some yards between themselves and the truck—an impulse of the central nervous system, perhaps. Maybe it takes a dense, primitive, Pleistocene brain to simply plod on. As we got lower in the canyon, the air cooled off, and we seemed to be suspended in a mesh of alternating light and shade.

There were plenty of vacancies at Ah-Di-Na Meadow campground, owing to the absence of any other campers. Deeds was overjoyed to have the place to himself. He sniffed around from campsite to campsite until he found one that satisfied him. It was close to the river. The river wasn't visible, though. We could just hear it, distantly. Deeds pulled the tarp from the truck bed, and we got the tent and set it up. We worked fast, because the light in the canyon was fading. The clock in the truck read four.

When we were done, and Deeds had hung the kerosene lantern from a branch, we suited up for fishing. The

McCloud had a lot of water in it for so late in the season. The water was fairly opaque, a silty green. It wasn't very wide at any point, because the sides of the canyon pinched it in, but it was still too deep for us to wade across. It had the classic configuration of a mountain trout stream. The fish would be in pockets behind boulders, in riffles, in sheltered pools, in slow stretches of water that echoed the serenity of Hat Creek. Once you've fished a few streams like the McCloud, you learn to skip quickly over the unproductive sections, just as you skip over slow passages in a book.

Deeds and I split up. He stayed below the campground, trying to coax a trout from a pool. I walked toward another pool downstream. I saw a hillside trail above me, but I decided to keep to the river, climbing over the rocks, outcrops, and deadfall, and bushwhacking through alders and cottonwoods. Suddenly, I stepped on a pinecone, lost my footing, and fell forward. My shinbone cracked against a hunk of granite. The blow broke my skin and gave me an instant hobble. I limped ahead to the pool. Trout were feeding actively. I tied on a small Adams—it's a good, all-purpose fly—and started casting. The casting was difficult, because the land behind me was a tangle of trees, bushes, and poison oak. The fish still came readily to the fly. They had none of the wariness of Hat Creek trout. They hadn't been subjected to the same kind of pressure. Before dark, I'd caught and released seven trout—all rainbows between eight and twelve inches long. They were average fish for the McCloud.

I wished I'd brought a flashlight for the walk back to the camp. I made some unnecessary detours before I found my way. Deeds was already cooking dinner. He had his two-

burner butane stove set on a folding table. Spuds were boil-
ing in one pot, and ground chuck was frying in the other.

"Do any good?" Deeds asked.

"I got quite a few. Nothing worth keeping."

"Same here." Deeds flipped over a hamburger. It
smelled terrific. I went over to warm my hands by the stove.

"There's only one burger in that pan," I said.

"I thought you were eating salad."

"Don't rub it in," I said.

Deeds fashioned another beef big-boy from his stash of
chuck, while I opened a beer and applied some ice from the
cooler to my wound. The bruise was entering an Abstract
Expressionist phase. It hurt. I pressed the beer can against
it, hoping that I hadn't also caught poison oak. Deeds saw
that I was hurting, and he carried the plate of burger and
boiled spuds over to me. We talked for a while about the
valley and our mutual friends and how their grapes and
prunes were doing. Deeds filled me in on deaths and births. I
told him how hard it had been for me to move away, since
the valley was where I'd learned to be at ease in nature. For
a long time, the solitude was a distinct pleasure, but then, all
at once, it had turned into isolation. He said that he understood; he still thought about selling his place when he was
feeling low. "It's romantic out there for a few years," he
said, slapping at a mosquito. "Then it just becomes regular
life." Deeds got up from his campstool and did the dishes.
His sleeping bag was in the tent. He attended to it fasti-
diously, fluffing the down, smoothing out the corners. There
wasn't any noise, except for the breeze in the firs and the
distant rumble of the river.

. . .

The highlight of our weekend in the canyon came on Saturday when Deeds caught a Dolly Varden on a caddis nymph he'd tied. Dolly Vardens are chars, not trout, but the resemblance is close. The fish have bright pink spots like the spots on the dress of their namesake, Dickens's Dolly Varden, who appears in *Barnaby Rudge*. In California, Dolly Vardens are almost extinct. The McCloud is the only river in which they've been rediscovered, so Deeds was pumped up by the fact that he'd hooked something unique. He held the fish in the sun and admired it for a few seconds before letting it go.

The best fishing we had was right where Deeds had predicted it would be—near the mouth of Ladybug Creek, just above the Nature Conservancy preserve. The conservancy is an organization whose sole purpose is to acquire and manage ecologically significant land. On the McCloud, it owns six-and-a-half miles of river frontage and 2,330 surrounding acres. Part of the preserve is open to the public, but we never visited it, because we had plenty of action in the less restricted wild trout water. Ladybug Creek—it's not much more than a trickle in autumn—serves as a prime feeding station for trout. As the creek tumbles down the canyon walls, over moss- and lichen-covered rocks, it washes insects into the McCloud, and the fish gather for an easy meal. We took them on wet flies and dry flies, on nymphs and streamers. We kept four of them for our Saturday night dinner. Deeds rubbed them with wild sage he found growing by the river and fried them in his familiar pan. I contributed the much discussed salad, which Deeds—in a move so out of character that it alarmed me—ate with enthusiasm.

Sunday morning I was awake before dawn. The throbbing in my shin had kept me from sleeping well. I heated some water for coffee and sat at the table just staring into space until I realized that I was cold. I put on a sweat shirt and warmed my hands in the steam that was billowing from the pot on the stove. The coffee Deeds had brought was freeze-dried. It tasted bitter to me, and I threw most of it on the ground. There was nothing to do but go fishing.

On every fishing trip, I reach a point of mechanization when the routine of each day becomes automatic, much like the routine of a commuter who has a regular train to catch. I trudged forward on my bad leg, down a trail to the river. It looked black. Not a stitch of light had hit it yet. The boulders I touched were chilly and damp. I came at last to a tongue of rock that extended into the river for ten or twelve feet. I took a nymph from my fly box, but my fingers were so stiff from the cold that I dropped it into the water. I watched it vanish, sucked downstream into some rapids. The second nymph I managed to tie on right. I cast it toward an alder on the opposite bank, then let it drift into the middle of the McCloud, quartering my line.

I must have been casting for twenty minutes before the sun finally rose. It struck me like a flame. In another twenty minutes, I was so warm that I stripped off my sweat shirt and tossed it on the rock. My casting fell into the hypnotic rhythm I'd been after at Hat Creek, obliterating conscious-ness, and I had one of those rare moments of epiphany that come when you're entirely open to them. I lost any sense of the McCloud as a specific river. It began to recapitulate every other river I'd fished, to exist briefly as an absolute form. The water stopped being merely water and became instead an adjunct of my body, so that I was joined to it in a steady flow. The moment didn't last very long, but that was all right. That was fine.

We broke camp late in the afternoon. Deeds judged the trip to be a success, even though he'd seen four other anglers during our stay. I enjoyed the canyon for its splendor and isolation, but I told Deeds that I wasn't ready to give up on the trout of Hat Creek. I wanted another shot at them someday—crowd or no crowd.

Our drive out was as rough as our drive in. We stopped at a bar in McCloud, and I bought Deeds a Diet Dr Pepper for the road. When the bartender asked if we'd been fishing or hunting, Deeds said, "Fishing," and then added, in the manner of a boy who has tried but failed to contain his pride, "I caught a Dolly Varden."

Driving back to San Francisco, I was uncommonly aware of traffic, blinking lights, complexity. I got home just before midnight. The punk rocker who'd rented the dilapidated studio apartment in the garage of my building was practicing his drums again. I'd made it clear to him before that he had to quit the drumming before somebody strangled him, so I was surprised that I was able to speak to him without feeling my hands twitching toward his throat. Upstairs, I ran myself a hot bath. I had a scratchy throat and a runny nose. The bruise on my shin had turned the exact color of an eggplant. On my forearms, I had a rash of pimples that looked suspiciously like poison oak. None of the damage really bothered me, though. Flesh matters so little to a happy man.